It's All About the Face

Quilted Fabric Portraits

By

Phyllis Cullen and Cindy Richard

ISBN: 978-1-7360544-0-6
Library of Congress Control Number: 2020922219

The information in this book is presented in good faith, but no warranty is given, nor results guaranteed concerning the level of success one may achieve through the use of the information contained herein. Although every effort was made to provide accurate information, Quilted Portraits and More, LLC, and the authors, Phyllis Cullen and Cindy Richard, assume no responsibility for any errors, inaccuracies, omissions, loss, damage or disruption resulting from negligence, accident or any other cause.

https://www.facebook.com/groups/itsallabouttheface
https://www.quiltedportraitsandmore.com
quiltedportraitsandmore@gmail.com

Dedication
To our parents

Phyllis's parents,
Milton and
Bernice Winer, z"l

Cindy's parents,
Leonard and
Nina Kaye

Acknowledgments

We want to thank our husbands for supporting this reach-for-the-stars project and our families who have been posing for us for years and never complained. Thanks to the inventors of Google Docs, magicJack®, WhatsApp, and Zoom, without which it would have been difficult to collaborate from opposite sides of the world. Thanks to our advisors and copy editors (including Mary Albin, Alani Cullen, Marc Cullen, Terence Cullen, Brian Garrison, Rivka Hamdani, Susanne Miller Jones, Hava Katzir, Molly Kaye, Mary Moody-Cox, Solveig Nordwall, Dassi Shani Pintar, David Richard, Frances Richard, Deborah Winer, Jeanne Winer, Adina Zuckerman.)
Thanks to Phyllis's excellent photographer, Randall Duryea.

Also, thanks to the members of our Facebook group, "It's All About the Face" (https://www.facebook.com/groups/itsallabouttheface), for their many suggestions, requests, postings of inspiring work, and allowing us, in many cases, to include their work to demonstrate our thoughts. And we'd like to thank our students who have been requesting a book like this since day one. Here is Book One. We hope it fills the need.

Table of Contents

Introduction

The highest form of art is the representation of the human face and figure. Art students through the ages have considered portraiture the most challenging subject. Quilters are no different.

After extensive research, we discovered there aren't any books on the market about how to quilt a fabric portrait. There are books that discuss thread painting. There are books that discuss how to sew around each patch of appliqué. There aren't any books about the best way to quilt portraits to emphasize anatomical contour and bone structure.

Many of us have attended classes where the focus was on a particular technique. At the end of the class, almost as an afterthought, the quilting and final touches were briefly covered. With one foot out the door, these most important details were often disregarded. "Quilt as desired" doesn't really work that well for portraits, at least in our opinion.

Our goal is to take you through the entire process of creating your own beautiful, amazing portraits. We will focus on layering techniques and the actual quilting of the portrait. We will also delve into anatomy, drawing, art principles, photography, composition, lighting, values, and the emotional aspects of people-centered art.

Whew. That's a lot! So we're breaking it up into two books. We don't want to skip any of the valuable information we've gathered, but we don't want anyone to get hurt lifting a single book.

Book One: "It's All About the Face"

Anatomy. To create a faithful, believable, and recognizable portrait, we think you should understand anatomy and how a face is structured. Where do bones protrude? Where are bones recessed? How do we replicate a person's likeness on a two-dimensional surface?

Photography. We will discuss taking a good reference photo to begin our story, and how lighting, composition, and posing are used to create a good photo.

Techniques. Making patterns. With the help of technology, we will explain the "nuts and bolts" of the digital process required for preparing a pattern so that you can convert your own photos into patterns.

Choosing fabrics. We will guide you through fabric choice by offering an in-depth explanation of color and value.

Making the quilt top. We'll explain two methods of collage in detail that provide all the steps to create a portrait you'll be proud of.

Quilting it. Most importantly, we will use lots of quilted examples to explain how to quilt for realism.

Texture. We'll introduce artists working in unusual fabric textures, such as printing or painting on fabric, thread painting, cheesecloth, and felting, to create realistic effects.

Telling a story. Since it is so important, we'll discuss our work's emotional content, using some of our favorite quilts and their stories to make our case.

Hand care. Phyllis (who is also a physician) explains how to care for our hands to reduce pain, because cutting and quilting puts stress on our hands.

Final touches and thoughts. The last chapter is a collection of tips we have accumulated that we really think will help you, from surface design to judging.

Book Two: "More than Just a Pretty Face"

Book Two will consist of three parts.

Part One: Going Deeper

We will continue our discussion about drawing and painting, understanding anatomy, perspective, composition and placing figures in situ, and depicting clothing. We will delve further into photography, discussing how to use modern camera features to upgrade our portraiture and learn hot tips from professional photographers about posing, lighting, and other digital tool options. Finally, we will tie together the historical evolution of portraiture and its myriad styles and genres with the current styles of fabric artists today.

Part Two: Beyond Realistic

There's a world of fun styles and techniques out there. We'll cover a range of examples, from abstract to surreal, by introducing you to the work of a number of amazing artists. We will show thread painting, printing on fabric, painting, embroidery, and varied textured examples from steel mesh to sheers. We won't worry about realism or believability. The sky's the limit!

Part Three: Animal Portraits

The last half of Book Two is for animal lovers. So let's create animal portraits! You will be able to build on the in-depth information in Book One, such as anatomy, composition, texture, embellishment and quilting, to create wild quilts of animals, birds, and bugs.

How to Use These Books

We expect most of you want to create faces, so dive right in. Book One will guide you through the entire process with all the comprehensive information provided. Once you get hooked, we believe you'll want to come along on the wilder exploration in Book Two.

You would have to do extensive research to accumulate the amount of information we have gathered here.

Phyllis Cullen

"Looking In"

I often hear "professional" artists insist that to be taken seriously, you have to find your "voice." I have concluded that one voice doesn't do it for me. I have never encountered an art medium or a style that I didn't like! Because so many types of different media appeal to me, it's hard to pick a favorite. Evidently, I am "multilingual."

That being said, if I had to pick, portraits and fabrics are my favorites. Certainly, because of my background as a physician, my interest is, above all, people. Knowledge of human anatomy, figure drawing, and portrait painting give me the tools to create portraits in any medium. There is something about bringing my subject to life in an unexpected medium that inspires me the most.

Why does a painter move on to "painting" with fabric? Well, besides the fun of shopping and fondling fabric(!), the textures, patterns, and dimensionality created by quilting multiple layers offer so many possibilities. I get a much richer effect by producing something tactile than I could ever achieve with photography, drawing, or painting.

Working with fabric can keep me occupied in the studio until 3 AM, while I manipulate thousands of colorful little pieces of cloth. I have experimented with and taught many portrait techniques. I have played it safe by painting or printing a face on fabric, and I have created wild collages with the most remarkable, often unexpected results.

And if I want, I can always add paint.

Best of all, I found that by beginning with well-composed, clear photos, and a little understanding of Photoshop®, I can create the basis for a fabric portrait. This approach has diverse possibilities, both for me and my students, who can now bring a subject to life with great reliability.

Lots of quilters have figured out the posterized-photo technique for making faces. However, many students fear they can't draw, are reluctant to learn anatomy or perspective, and especially fear they will ruin their portraits when they try to quilt them.

I want you to set aside these fears. I am certain that if you put in the effort, they are all learnable skills. Besides, the physician in me wants to remind you that we are, after all, doing all this for FUN. A wrong stitch will not lead to infection, bleeding, or an open wound!

My greatest satisfaction is finding that adding details with quilting lines really pulls the piece together, but is considered the most challenging part of the process. So let's meet that challenge in this book.

Take a deep breath and pull up a chair. Enjoy the journey. This will be fun.

Phyllis Cullen Fine Art
(http://www.phylliscullenartstudio.com)

8

Cindy Richard

"Happy at 60"

I started quilting as a lark. It was a way to pass the time while raising young kids and working a full-time, highly technical job. I took a basic class with a local teacher and immediately fell in love with everything about the quilting process: the fabric, the color, the texture. It quickly morphed from a passing hobby to a passion for which it seems there is never enough time. I have to be pried out of my studio at the end of the day, or I would forget to eat or sleep.

My quilting experience quickly progressed from traditional to quilt art. Although I was very excited at the beginning just to play with fabrics, I soon realized that geometric shapes weren't going to hold my interest for too long. I found a quilt guild and started to attend meetings. I surfed internet sites to learn as much as I could about everything quilted. I dreamt about my quilt projects and bought fabric like it was candy. I traveled to quilt exhibits for inspiration, and then I found quilted portraits.

Phyllis Cullen came to our guild to teach, and I enrolled in her portrait class. My practice piece was based on a photo of my parents. (It's the quilt in the dedication.) Phyllis told us to bring dark, medium, and light valued fabrics. We used labels and fusing to assemble the tops. It was brilliant. In minutes I could see my dad's eyes looking back at me. As if by magic, I walked into the world of portraiture.

Since my first experience with fabric portraits, I have been studying portrait drawing and painting with a local artist who taught me how to bring the human face alive on a flat surface. This knowledge enabled me to improve my fabric portraits. But the final step in creating quilted faces lies in quilting them. Quilting isn't just the glue; it isn't just an enhancement or the bling; it is part of the whole, harmonized composition. The quilting follows the shapes under the skin and gives the subject form.

In my very methodical way of learning more and improving my skill, I sought tutorials, videos, books, and articles about quilting faces, but I did not find anything of substance. I found many techniques about creating the top, but quilting portraits was not covered in depth. I called Phyllis, and I told her we had a new project to work on. We would need to write the book ourselves. And that is how this book was born!

CindyRQuilts.com
(https://www.CindyRQuilts.com)

9

1 Why Do It in Fabric?

We are attracted to images of human and animal faces. We are drawn in by thought-provoking responses evoking emotion and passion. Expressive faces speak to something very primal within us. They harken back to our first focused image of our mothers' faces in a way that even the loveliest landscape or still life cannot do. Portraits are people with whom we must interact. We are compelled to divine their thoughts, feelings, personalities, and histories from the expressions on their faces and their body language.

To artists, the human figure represents the epitome of challenge and satisfaction. For some of us, to produce a recognizable likeness is most gratifying. Portraits are created in all styles and genres, from very abstract to simplified, from garish to monotone, from distorted cubist to wildly colored Fauvist. And some of us love these less conventional options! Each style is deliberately chosen to express and evoke a feeling, a response, an understanding of the subject's essence. The purpose may vary from honoring a saint to caricaturing an enemy.

We are fascinated by all the permutations of the human form. We try to capture it in every medium. We are fabric artists. We are Artists! The debate rages on. Is working in fabric completely different, or is it simply a different art medium with the same rules and art principles?

We believe fiber art is on par with painting in oil, watercolor, pastel, pencil, or ink as a fine art form, but with several important advantages. Fabric can feature a printed or woven surface design for visual texture in addition to color and value. The world of fiber is endless and includes a medley of actual textures, such as smooth cotton and silk, fluffy wool and felt, coarse linen, subtle tulle and organza, and sparkling Angelina® fibers. It's no wonder art quilts have a three-dimensional quality, as the combined stitched layers add actual dimension as well.

These advantages make fabric our medium of choice, or we wouldn't be here.

To create a realistic portrait in any medium requires using lines and shapes, and emphasizing contours to render a three-dimensional subject on a flat surface. As fabric artists, we need to know the rules of proportions and perspective, especially if we are going to break them or transcend them. This is a topic we'll explore in this book as well as in Book Two, "More than Just a Pretty Face."

Masters like Rembrandt and Vermeer used light and dark values to define features and create dimension. Light and shadow, shading, the use of value, blending, and color all assist in the process. These artists created smooth transitions between colors and values by blending their oil paints. Quilt artists have to blend pieces of fabric and use correctly placed quilting threads to achieve similar results.

"Benjamin Franklin," Phyllis

The basic elements of art apply to every medium, including fabric. The bits of fabric are the first "dabs of paint," and the quilting lines provide the details. By using fabrics of light and dark values, we can play with light and shadows to create depth and perspective.

An axiom in art is that value is more important than color. That axiom applies equally to fabric art. Value is a cornerstone that we will be emphasizing a lot. When you use value properly, the result is believable, even if the most unrealistic colors, patterns, and textures are used.

The charcoal and pencil works of great artists were quite believable. Color was not needed for master artists who worked in charcoal, like Leonardo da Vinci.

This book will take you through the highlights of the portrait process. However, the quilt top alone is not where the story ends.

Our process begins with a photo of a face and what it means to take a good photo: choosing, posing, and shooting a good reference photo.

Look at this photo. What do you see? There is a story being told by this couple. Their mood is playful and happy.

Reference photo, Phyllis

Understanding the principles of anatomy and facial proportions is important, but what if you can't draw? We have a secret weapon—digital technology. We use a photo-editing program, like Adobe Photoshop®, to help manipulate the image. Then, guided by the resulting posterized version of the image, we add and subtract many multicolored bits of fabric organized by value until the main features are formed.

Fabric choices help us create the effect we desire—realistic or impressionistic, whimsical or muted. We use texture, prints, colors, and values to express our vision and make our work unique. Finally, the layers are fused into a collage.

"Lovebirds Two,"
Unquilted, Phyllis

The principles of art are the backbone for constructing features. If a shape, color, fabric, texture, or quilting pattern doesn't work, it could ruin the desired effect. Because fabrics do not blend like paints, stitching is used to blend fabric edges and create transitions. Quilting adds texture and detail to create the contours. No matter what, the quilting lines can make or break the illusion of a recognizable composition.

That's why an understanding of anatomy is important. Bone structure creates the planes and angles of the face, which are common to all. Muscle and soft tissue give us unique features. By adding stitching along the lines of the underlying bone structure (after adding lights and shadows using value), we can turn a generic face into a real likeness to our original photo.

Quilting the portrait brings it all together. See for yourself. Here is the same portrait after quilting. Can you see how the quilting enhances, unifies, adds depth, dimension, and fully enhances the believability of the portrait?

"Lovebirds Two," Phyllis

Ready? Let's get started!

From an Artist's Point of View

The Skull

Nature is composed of cubes, cones, spheres, and cylinders. Everything is a variation of these shapes. Bones form the skeletal structure. Let's consider the skull, which like the rest of our body, consists of "hills and valleys." The skull is shaped like a sphere and is divided into elements. The forehead or brow (hill) overlooks the eye sockets (valleys) between which is the nose (hill). The cheekbones and jawbone (hills) are the highlands that border the face. The mouth occupies the valley between the outer edges of the jawbone. Muscles and cartilage fill in the cavities. Lips (hills), made of soft tissue, protrude.

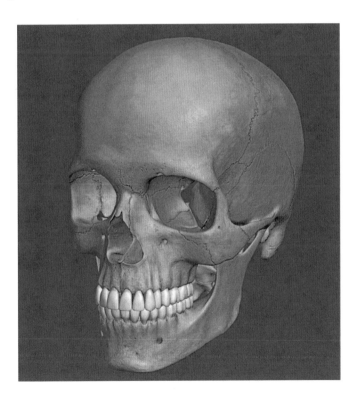

The Human Form

The body is an assemblage of hills and valleys. If we consider the human form from top to bottom, the neck, shoulders, ribs, and pelvis all radiate from a central cylindrical spine. The bones give structure to the human form enabling it to stand erect, as they protect the internal organs and muscles. The bones give shape (hills) to the form. The valleys fill in the soft spaces between the bones. Clothing drapes over this composite, showing off its shape and beauty.

Face It! Portrait Rules

Let's see how a face is structured. We are not going to teach you to draw a face, although that is a great skill to have. Understanding the face's anatomy will help you interpret the facial features so that your portrait will be accurate and realistic if you want it to be—and believable in any case. You'll know if it doesn't look right, and more importantly, how to fix it.

This drawing by Phyllis shows the expression of a one-eyed man looking up at an angle.

"Greek Hero," Phyllis

When you look at a photo of a face, do you really "see" where all the features are so that you can recreate them on a two-dimensional surface? Ultimately you will need to train yourself to really pay attention to what you are seeing. Are you looking at the face at eye level, or are you gazing up or down at it? Which features align horizontally? Which features are in front? Which are behind? The compilation of blended features forms a face made of raised skeletal bones and recesses between these bones.

If you look at a drawing where the features are not arranged according to the acceptable proportions, scale, or position, you immediately recognize something is off with that drawing. It should make you feel uncomfortable looking at it. (Perhaps the artist has done this deliberately, but that's another story.)

Step one is knowing when it isn't right. How do we know? We look at bone structure to see where the bones protrude outward and where they sink in. Since shading is used to emphasize recessed features, we need to know which parts to shade when depicting a face.

Step two is knowing some of the guidelines that artists apply in rendering a face. Imagine you have a flat map that shows you where facial features are in relation to each other. We could call these "ideal" features (even though most of us do not have perfect proportions).

Actually, those deviations from the "ideal" create the individual characteristics of each person, and it is by noting them and reproducing them that we capture a likeness of that person.

We are all unique. Most of us are not perfectly symmetrical—our eyes are not exactly aligned horizontally. Some eyes are close together, and others are farther apart. The shape and color of eyes vary. Noses, chins, and ears are also very individual and come in many sizes and shapes. The same can be said about the shape of a smile. Features also vary significantly according to age and gender.

Replicating a person's likeness on a two-dimensional surface will result in achieving a recognizable subject. But, if the nose is too small or not in exactly the right place, that rendering will not look like the person you want to recreate.

"Lady Feather" actually began as a drawing. The artist chose to use a gradation of values and more or less contoured quilting, but with a less blended and more graphic approach. She used a high-key value scheme to endorse the lovely fairy tale quality of the subject.

"Lady Feather," Nancy Turbitt

Lura Schwarz Smith is an artist who feels at home drawing on paper or fabric. The quilted line supports the composition.

*Detail of "Seams a Lot Like Degas,"
Lura Schwarz Smith*

Ages and Gender Alter a Face

Have you ever considered why children are cuter than adults? Children have round faces with big, round eyes, which are spread wide apart, and small noses. All these round, smooth-skinned facial characteristics create a pleasing appearance.

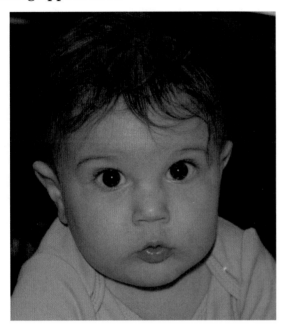

Elderly adult faces tend to have heavier eyelids, longer noses, larger ears, thinner lips, and wrinkles. Their faces are not as round as children's faces, making them less cute. Even if they're smiling!

Male faces often have less space between the eyes and brows. Their ears and noses tend to be larger, and their brows are heavier than those of females. Male noses and chins are often more prominent and angular than their female counterparts. Larger eyes, fuller lips, and rounder/oval jawbones are frequently considered feminine traits.

Eyes, Noses, Lips, and Teeth

It is said that "Eyes are the window to the soul." Happiness, sadness, pensiveness, and truth can all be sensed by peering into someone's eyes.

With eyes that are closed, very shadowed, or covered by glasses, we can still create a successful piece of art, but seeing the eyes provides us with more information about the inner person.

Accurately depicted eyes are crucial to the success of your art. There are generally accepted principles to follow for all eyes. The upper lid, which sticks out more than the lower lid, should overlap the iris and pupil. There is a slight shadow below the upper eyelid. The eye's cornea is slightly off-white or peachy and gets darker toward the corners of the eye. There is a tear duct in each corner closest to the nose. Eyelashes on the upper lid are fuller than those on the bottom lid. Eyebrows vary, but there is a curved direction to the hairs that follow the shape of the brow. The brow is a high point on the skull and is typically in light compared with the eyes, which are recessed, and therefore in shadow.

Pay attention to the shape of the eye, which can be round, oval, triangular, or even diamond-shaped. Eyes come in different colors and shades of blue, green, brown, and black. Many times the shapes of eyes and the coloring of the iris are influenced by race or genetics. The shape of the eye looks very different depending on the angle from which it is viewed. Within the lids, the shape of the eyeball is rounded. You want to show that roundness using shadowing along the edges.

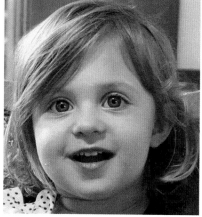

From a frontal view, the iris and pupil are both round. Their shape becomes more oval or stretched from an angular view, but the pupil is always round and centered within the iris. The eye's apparent shape is also altered by the facial expression, as seen in these examples.

Notice the position of the iris, and how much iris you can actually see. The top and bottom of the iris are often truncated, so you do not see any white below or above the iris. The iris typically resembles a fine starburst, with lines radiating from the pupil. A spot of light touches the pupil and iris, giving life to the eye. This reflective spot of light, called a catchlight, is in the same place on both eyes and is on the side of the light source.

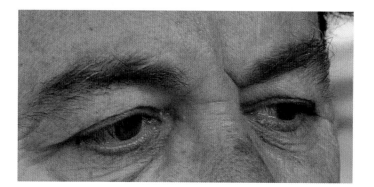

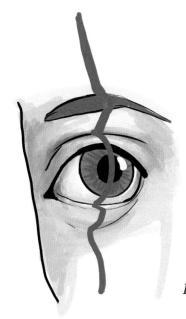

Eye, Molly Kaye

In this example, the blue line running through the eye area helps define the structure. The eyebrow follows the bony contour of the brow, thus making the name "eyebrow" entirely appropriate. You can see from the shading that the area below the eyebrow recedes. This area is usually in shadow, including the upper lid. The upper lid of the eye stretches upward toward the nose and forehead, while the lower lid drops down toward the outer side of the face. The edge of the lower lid is facing up and is usually very light. Remember, eyes sit in shadow in a recessed socket surrounded by brow and bones.

The baby's eyes show very little of the lids and appear rounder, but are shaded under the brow nonetheless. The older eyes have prominent lids covering more of the eyeball, especially when squinting into the light. Wrinkles leading away from the eye characterize grandpa, not baby with those full chubby cheeks!
In this example of an older man, notice the laugh lines around his eyes, which go hand in hand with the smile lines around his mouth.

The Nose

Noses vary in size and shape, but their anatomical makeup is always the same. The bridge of the nose is bone. The balance of the nose is cartilage, which widens into a bulb shape at its tip. Both the bridge and the tip appear as lighter areas because they protrude from the face. Nostrils, which are recessed holes, are shadowed and dark.

If you view a nose from an angle, the nose will block the light, causing a shadow on its far side. The side closest to you will be lighter. Shading next to the nose will help develop the proper shape.

Notice the shadows on the sides of the nose, as well as the highlights on the bridge and tip. Nostrils may not be very apparent unless the nose or the face is upturned. On the woman's face in this photo, notice the highlights on the protruding areas, such as cheeks, front of the lower lip, chin, and forehead. By using lighter values in drawing, painting, or fabric selection, you can reproduce these highlights to create perspective and volume.

To understand the contours of a nose, use your finger to follow the shape of your nose. Begin mid-cheek and follow a line towards the nose.

Climb over your nose and continue to the other cheek. If you were to draw your finger's discovery path, the result would be a curved line with an abrupt bulge in the middle. This bump is a lot like a cone, which is the basic shape of every nose. If you follow another line over the nostrils, it's more like a gradual climb. Begin mid-cheek, progress over a nostril, then over the bulb of the nose. Descend over the second nostril and finally stop at the second cheek.

This exercise will help you delineate the form of the nose and really understand the bone structure. Once you can visualize this in your mind's eye, you will be able to draw it and also quilt it.

Lips: More than a Frown or Smile

In this smiling face in the quilt close-up, we see a lot of activity. Notice the shadow beside the nose and the dark nostrils. Note the interior of the mouth and the teeth. The deeper they are in the mouth, the darker they appear. If the teeth did not change value, the mouth would look flat, like piano keys.

Detail of "Lovebirds 2-4 Love," Phyllis

Lips vary in shape and size. Some lips are more prominent than others, but there is no mistaking a frown for a smile. The upper lip spreads, lifts, and straightens when a person smiles. Also, laugh-lines form, as previously mentioned. Because the bottom lip protrudes more than the top lip, the bottom lip's center is typically lighter and as we see in the photo, often actually includes a spot of reflected light.

Lips cover the fronts of curving jaws, so they are convex, not flat. The top lip's shape has a downward curve in the center, sometimes called a Cupid's bow when it is prominent. The cleft above the top lip, running from nose to lips, which is called the philtrum, is also recessed and in shadow. The area between the bottom lip and the chin is recessed. The shadow in the recess is called a form shadow. There is a fine, light-colored border at the edges of the lips where they meet the skin.

Lips have a vertical grain. If we follow the point of convergence of these grained lines, it would be deep inside the mouth. The corner edges of the lips, where they join, are dark shadowed areas.

When lips are parted, you can see into the mouth, which appears dark because it is recessed and in shadow. If lips are open, you can see teeth, which are lighter colored, fading to slightly darker as they recede into the corners of the mouth, since the jaw's shape is sort of a horseshoe. Only the teeth directly in the line of light will be brightly lit.

Try This

This is an exercise you can do before beginning any project. Use your fingertips to trace the bone structure of your face, which has seven hills and valleys as we cross from one side of the head to the other. Follow the hills and valleys to remind yourself how they slope, where they are positioned, and how they are shaped. It will help keep the anatomy real for you. Learn all the contours so that they are intuitive when you begin working.

Why is a portrait more compelling by its very nature than flowers or scenery or architecture? We think it's because the best photos are personal and they tell a story.

Top photographers have ways to personalize a photograph:

- Add humor or something surprising
- Include mystery or a puzzling aspect
- Show an opinion or a point of view
- Include human drama by putting a person in the photo, even if the primary inspiration was a beautiful sunset

Since we are focusing on portraits, and therefore featuring living beings (people and animals both count), we are way ahead of the game. The challenge is to convert them into artwork and make them "pop."

Start with a good reference photo. Ideally, we want to work with a high-resolution, high-contrast photo for our project. (After you have some experience, you will find you can bend this guideline a bit because we don't always have ideal photos.)

For a classic portrait, we start with a close-up of a headshot with shoulders. Soft natural lighting near a window will provide a reliably good result and the most detail on the face of your subject.

If you are using artificial light, look for interesting sources, not just overhead lighting. Try using a crack in the window shade or a glowing candle between lovers. You get the idea. However, try to have only one light source or the shadows will be confusing.

Shooting a Reference Photo

Whether you are posing your subject or looking for one to use among those you have, there are certain considerations.

The ultimate goal is to take a crisp enough photo so that when it is enlarged to full size (the same size as the quilt), the details will be clear and sharp. Don't compromise on missing details. If the subject has moved or an element is hidden, retake the photo.

Use a tripod, or else lean on the back of a chair or a wall to help keep the camera steady, so your photo will be sharp. Many newer cameras have lens stabilization that can help as well. Look for these features to help you produce a clear image. **We just can't emphasize enough how critical it is to start with a sharp image.**

If we want a classic portrait that fills the frame, we need a close-up shot. In taking a photo to use as a reference, let's not take a photo of a subject in the distance and enlarge it or crop a face out of a crowd of people. Too much detail in the features will be sacrificed.

For a classic headshot, get as close to the subject as possible and fill the viewfinder frame with the face. When taking portrait photos, limit the photo to the entire head, from the top of the head until just below the shoulders. Even if you want to place the person in a supporting scene, try to limit the scope so that the subject extends from top to bottom.

It's actually a good idea to take a close-up to get the details of the subject. If you aren't going to place your subject in a different setting, take several more shots of the entire scene you will be using. By taking photos of the whole scene, you'll have the correct direction of light and shadow. The subject and background can't be lit differently, or the effect will be very jarring and look very wrong.

Telling an Original Story

If you can, use a photo you've taken yourself, instead of borrowing someone else's idea. You will find great satisfaction in a work that is totally your own creation. Even if you get permission to use someone else's photo, you are borrowing someone else's emotional inspiration. (Besides, the minefields of copyright rules are not pleasant to navigate.)

Emotion or storytelling begins when you capture a moment you want to remember. The background may be beautiful, but does it enhance or detract from your subject? You may be better off blurring the background if you want to concentrate on the interaction between lovers or a mother and child, for example. You may want to crop away any extraneous detail that doesn't add to the message. Change your point of view by standing on a chair or kneeling down. Zoom in close. Sometimes having the action continue off the edge of the photo adds tension and has a dramatic effect. The goal is to grab and hold the attention of the viewers and help them feel the energy in that captured moment.

This oil painting by Phyllis shows the effect of zooming in on the subject. By simplifying and blurring the background, attention is locked onto the subject. The interaction between mother and child needs no special setting. This example is typical of classic portraiture.

"Mother's Love," Phyllis

In the next quilt by Cindy, the very simple background is effective, because attention is placed on the interaction between the expressions and body language of the boy and his grandfather with the book they are reading together.

"Discovery," Cindy

There are common lists of advice and suggestions offered by many photographers about taking a good shot. Here are a few of the ideas:

- How do we make our subjects look their best? Pose them appropriately!
- To enhance the appearance of a female subject, fashion photographers will often have the model turn her body away from the camera, and then turn her face at a three-quarter angle towards the camera.
- Encourage a female subject to keep her arms away from her body, so she doesn't look larger.
- Tell her to lean back, bend one knee, and glance upward with her head tilted to the side while appearing as if she has a reason to do so.
- A male subject evokes strong "masculinity"

if his pose is nearly a profile, with his eyes turned to the camera, leaning a bit forward with his arms at his sides.

This photograph by Phyllis demonstrates an interesting and out-of-the-ordinary pose for a family portrait that follows these guidelines.

The interaction between a couple can be shown by touching or having them look or lean in toward each other. If you are photographing a couple kissing, the advice is to shoot over the man's shoulder, so her nose is in front of his, and her face is upturned to the camera. In any event, if you can catch a couple in a playful moment that demonstrates their feelings for each other, go for that, regardless of the lighting or background.

Lighting

Lighting is probably the foremost consideration in the enhancement of a portrait. Wedding, fashion, and portrait photographers suggest that subjects face the light. If you are in sunlight and the light is coming from above, try to have your subject lift up his/her chin to avoid a shadow on the lower part of the face. Tilting the head to the side also creates a reflection of light on the cheek that is turned slightly away from the light. Backlighting is great for adding drama to a scene, thin rays of light, such as a slit of light from window blinds or a pool of light from a street sign can also add ambience, while the background is blurred.

The entire scene may be set with choice lighting conditions to provide atmosphere and contrast. Dark skies can add a somber ambience (though you may risk missing facial details for your quilt). Stormy clouds can evoke danger and make the viewer feel edgy, or they can be light and fluffy and simply make the sky look more interesting. Clouds in a sunset sky add wonderful color.

If you take photos at the end of the day or early in the morning during the so-called golden hours, the sun's rays create warm highlights and long deep shadows.

Sunny, bright photos suggest a happy and light setting. But be careful in full sunlight, especially when the light is coming from behind your subject. You may need to add light to your subject's face to avoid loss of detail. Bright sunlight is the most challenging natural light in terms of creating atmosphere. There are no shadows and subjects may appear harsh, even when you have them facing the light.

If the subject of your quilt is a still, posed figure photographed indoors, use one natural light source from a window to take the photo. Avoid competing light sources that introduce a lot of shadows.

Try not to use overhead lights or a flash, which can be very harsh and flatten the subject. These lights interfere with the shadows that distinguish facial features.

This photo was taken with a flash. The result is a beautiful portrait but if you try to posterize it, it will appear very flat because there are no shadows.

Poses with an odd tilt or with your subject looking up without an apparent reason will cause your portrait to look weird. Try to avoid such poses, at least initially. With greater experience in painting or digital manipulation, there are ways to improve them, but it's exhausting and time consuming. Trust us, it's always better to take a good picture in the first place, rather than to face the challenges of post processing.

The more values from light to dark within the face, the easier it will be to depict a 3D image of a face in the digital pattern. Side lighting, rather than light from the front or above, often creates the best pattern of shadows.

If the light is emanating from behind the subject, likely you will have a silhouette without seeing the subject's defining features.

Other guidelines suggest not placing an object or subject at the edge of the photo. Instead, let the subject extend virtually, past the border. Try not to cut your subject's limbs off awkwardly—either below the elbow or below the knee.

Composition ◊

Where should the focal point appear in your composition? The safest rule of composition is to use the "rule of thirds," which means a picture is divided into thirds both vertically and horizontally. Some of these intersecting imaginary lines that divide the picture should cross through the subject's face, so it receives the attention it is due. This will place the subject off center, which is more interesting than dead center. We will discuss more about composition in Book Two.

What is the mood you want the photo to convey? Is there harmony and a sense of peace in the picture? Assuming the photo is meant to create harmony, is the photo successful? Is there disharmony built into the scene intentionally to make the viewer edgy? This could also work well, if unease is the emotion you want to evoke.

Be mindful that the subject is in proportion to the setting and the overall size of the photo. The main subject should not be too far away or it will be too small to recreate in a quilt. If the face of the subject in a photo is larger than life, the photo sometimes may be overwhelming. However, because our final product is a quilt, rather than a photo, large faces afford more detail and are often quite effective when they are life size or larger.

When taking a photo, it's a good idea to remove any distractions that detract from the focus. Remove that gum wrapper, broomstick, or garbage can from the scene. We can crop them out later, before making our quilt pattern, but they may leave unwanted and unexplained shadows on the subject. It's always easier to work from a clean photo if possible. In addition, in our quilts, we have the freedom to change the background and place our subjects just where we want them.

As reference for your final photo, take lots of different angles of the same scene. Shoot the photo from above, below, and from the side, while keeping the lighting in mind. Zoom in and out on details of the scene so you can refer to different aspects of the scene while you are creating the quilt.

Foreshortening

Whatever feature is closest to the camera will appear larger or out of proportion, and not necessarily how we want to portray our subject. For example, a prominent nose may appear enlarged.

The solution is not to ignore the distortion, because then we will try to "fix" it according to what we "think" we see, and not according to what we "do" see. When we view a figure in different poses or from sharp angles rather than straight on, we have to depict it on the flat surface with a rule of linear perspective, called foreshortening. Because of the exaggerated angle, the length of a limb may be decreased, and the size of a hand or foot may need to be greatly increased in size to maintain a realistic effect. Depending on the angle of view, the hand or foot will appear very large up close and will elongate and narrow at its farthest end. This view is of course an illusion just like other forms of perspective.

Keep this in mind when taking your photo. Try

to bend down to the level of your subject if you are photographing a child, so you do not end up with this unusual perspective or that really big nose.

This quilt by Cindy shows the deliberate use of foreshortening to create a realistic pose of the two men in the air. Notice the tiny feet nearly hidden behind them.

"Flight," Cindy

Camera or Cellphone?

Nowadays cellphones and cameras can be used interchangeably to take reasonably good, high resolution photos. It isn't our goal to tell you to go out and buy a new, expensive camera. Eventually the technology of cellphones will catch up to that of good cameras.

Of course there are many things to consider in good photography, including all the camera settings, lighting and setting options, backgrounds, composition, etc. We will be dealing with many of these considerations in the sections on photography and composition in Book Two but we did want to touch on them here.

23

And... the Caveat

We will always tell you to try for the clearest, best photo you can take upon which to base your quilt art. But if you have an emotional attachment to a particular photo, even if it isn't of great quality and even if it is a little blurry, we would tell you to give it a try. It may be a more challenging experience because it will be harder to see the minute details clearly, but we would encourage you to follow your heart. There will be an example of this and some thoughts on dealing with this issue later in this book.

4 Quilt Pattern Design

Once you have chosen a photo as the basis for your realistic portrait, you need to make a pattern of the photo. We will describe a process using digital tools.

Using Technology to Make a Pattern

We find that technology makes this process much easier and more accurate. We utilize photo-editing software to manipulate and then posterize the photo. First, let's discuss how this technology relates to working with our image.

Value: The Key to a Posterized Pattern

We begin by discussing value, because the basis for photo-editing software is the detection and separation of values.

The value of a color (how light or dark it is) is the direct effect of how much light is reflected.

In monochromes, value is the range from white to gradually darkening grays and finally to black. In a multicolored composition the same gradation of value exists—from lightest to darkest with midtones in between.

A face is shaped like an egg. Lit from above, the forehead would be the lightest value and the chin would be darkest. In between, ignoring the features, the values would become progressively darker the farther away they are from the light source. If the light is coming from the side, the same thing happens. The closer cheek would be lightest, while the opposite cheek would be darkest in value.

In any color or combination, the lightest values are nearly white, or very "pastel." Conversely, the darkest value would be close to black. By studying a color photo, desaturating it into black and shades of gray, and then using posterizing tools, we can separate a photo into light, medium, and dark values. These values help us translate what we are seeing. Dark values appear in shadows and in recessed areas (valleys) of the face, like eye sockets. Lighter values appear where light is hitting a raised surface (hills), like the tip of a nose or even a cheekbone. We build our portraits by combining these layers into a composite, while using the original photo as a guide.

Levels

In the demonstrations of creating a digitally assisted pattern, we use "levels" (a photo editing term for values) to separate the areas of the face or body into values from light to dark. Instead of an artist eyeing these levels, the software determines them. This can be very helpful in deciding how dark or light any plane is, relative to adjacent planes. Each plane catches the light differently depending on the light source and the position of the head.

We will use the following digital tools to manipulate our photo for this technique before touching any fabric:

1. Desaturating the photo into black & white and shades of gray
2. Using a histogram to review the contrasting values
3. Sharpening the contrast of the photo and optimizing details by manipulating the histogram
4. Posterizing into layers

There are several programs and applications available for photo editing that do the basic required functions. We will explain the process using our favorite tool, Adobe® Photoshop® Elements 2020. If you want to use another program, follow these basic procedures using the program you choose.

For more information, visit the sites provided. Make sure your operating system supports the program you select. Check for tutorials about how to use the many available features.

Adobe® Photoshop® Elements 2020, a scaled-down version of the full-scale Adobe® Photoshop program, is ample for our purposes. You can purchase it for a one-time cost. It is supported by Windows and Mac®.
https://www.adobe.com/products/photoshop-elements.html

GIMP™ (GNU Image Manipulation Program) calls itself a "Free & Open Source Image Editor." It is free to use.
https://www.gimp.org/

Adobe® Photoshop® CC, full version is geared toward graphics professionals. This version is subscription-based. Supported by Microsoft® Windows and Apple® Mac products. Tablets with Windows 10 and iPad Pro® with iOS 14 support Photoshop CC.

https://www.adobe.com/products/photoshop.html

We prefer working on a PC or Mac, because we did not find suitable programs specific to tablets or cellphones that serve our purposes. (Although you can run Photoshop CC on your Android™ device if you have installed Windows 10.)

If you are bent on photo editing on a mobile device, check out Photo Art for Android and AFFINITY® Photo for Apple® iPad®. If you start with an optimally created photo, you might get away with using it. Although these are optional programs, it would be easier and more efficient if you did what we are going to explain in this chapter on your PC or Mac.

What Does Photo Editing Do for Us? (a Caveat)

We have discussed value in depth, because you need to understand this concept intuitively. The idea behind using a tool like Elements is to make it easier to distinguish slight variations in value. However, using these tools is not meant to be a crutch. You can't just rely on the program to do all the work for you. You have to make the value changes appropriately at the curves of the features. You have to be able to distinguish the separation of features even when there is no value change in the posterized pattern. Too often people use the shapes created by posterizing without understanding that the anatomy (shapes of the features) has to be considered as well.

Understanding the concept of value enables us to use technology to create a portrait without actually being an expert in drawing or photography.

While using Elements, evaluate the effect at each step to see if it works and will look realistic using layers of fabric.

Always remember to keep the original photo handy, so you can refer to it and understand what you are looking at, while working with your posterized version.

Ok, let's get started!

We will look at some images to help explain what makes a good photo for this process and how to manipulate a photo to get it to work better if the original version is too light or too dark.

We will use three examples in detail and show how to deal with common issues as we explain the process step by step.

Photo Editing with Adobe Photoshop Elements 2020

If you have an earlier version of Elements, the menu choices below may be slightly different, but the steps are the same.

Photoshop really offers many ways to do the same task. This can be confusing. So we are going to show you the simplest and most direct methods to accomplish your goal. However, if you learn the program and see another way that makes more sense to you, go for it.

Opening Your Image

From Adobe Photoshop Elements 2020, import the image you want to open.

First Image

1. Elements offers three modes: Quick, Guided, and Expert. Using **Expert** mode, select the image. We will be working with a photo of Danielle in these steps.

First Image, step 1

2. Select **Layer** > **Duplicate Layer**. Now your original image is part of the history and you can refer back to it as you work.

First Image, step 2

3. Crop the image so your subject appears as you want it to be in your quilt. We are not concerned with the background, only the subject's face and shoulders. You will decide on the background at another stage of this process.

Desaturating to Black & White

4. From the toolbar at the top of the window, select **Enhance** > **Convert to Black and White** to desaturate the image.

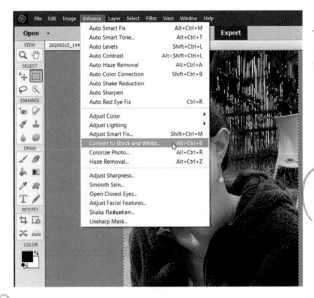

First Image, step 4

5. View the black & white styles. Click on each style until you select the one with the highest contrast. "Portraits" may not have the most contrast.

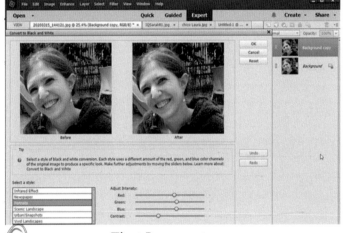

First Image, step 5

6. Once you have made your selection, click **OK**. The desaturated (black & white) version of the image opens.

First Image, step 6

Contrast and Histogram

7. At the top of the column on the right there is a row of icons. Select 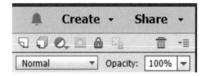 **(split ring icon)** to manipulate the contrast.

First Image, step 7

8. Select **Levels** to view the corresponding histogram, which shows the gradations of dark to light in the image.

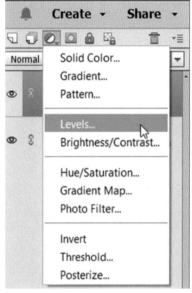

First Image, step 8

Histograms are graphical representations of the range of values in an image, ranging from darkest (left side) to lightest (right side). The shape of the histogram does not represent objects in the image. The histogram is a distribution of the number of pixels of each value. The higher peaks show us there are more pixels of that value in the image.

When a photo is well-balanced, the graph is centered along the horizontal (x) axis. The peaks along the vertical (y) axis tell us how much concentration of each value appears in the image.

9. This is the histogram for the image we have been viewing. Notice under the graph there are three arrows. The numbers beside the arrows represent their locations along the x-axis. By moving the arrows we can shift the concentration of the values, which changes the contrast of the image.

As a guide, it is ideal if the left arrow is at the 0 position and the middle arrow is under the highest peak. In this histogram the middle arrow is around 1.00, which is a good place to start. Adjustments to the histogram are intuitive, rather than an exact science. You always want to pay attention to the detail around the eyes. Watch the image as we move the arrows until there is contrast around the eyes.

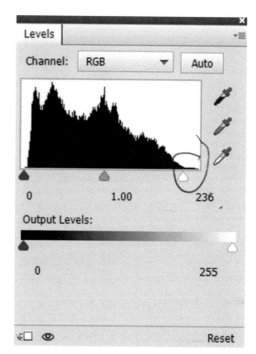

First Image, step 10

Overall this is a well-balanced photo and requires very little manipulation. If you still need to increase the contrast, while moving the arrows, pay attention to the area around the eyes.

Tip: In some cases the resulting histogram might be too light or too dark. You will be able to control the contrast of the face better if you select only the face, rather than the entire image before creating the histogram. See the Third Image.

If you do not like the changes you have made, click **Reset** and start again (or **Edit** > **Undo**).

Note: Be sure when you are using the layer manipulating split-circle tools or filters that you are working on the correct layer. Each time you change levels or contrast, etc., another layer will appear in the layer panel. When you want to manipulate the image, click on the layer showing the image itself. It's easy to think your program isn't working when you aren't on the correct layer.

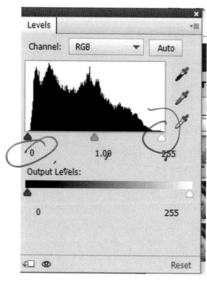

First Image, step 9

10. The right arrow should be under the graph where it starts to rise.

Move the right arrow to where the graph starts to rise, in this case, **236**. Press **Enter**.

Posterizing

11. Once you are satisfied that the contrast is saturated and rich enough, select  > **Posterize**.

Choose between 4–6 levels so the result includes a wide range of values, from very light, med light, med dark, and very dark. Adjust the levels until you are satisfied with the range of values and the amount of detail provided by the overlap of levels. You want to create a pattern with recognizable features.

There is no recipe for the number of required levels. Sometimes 4 levels look better than 6 levels. Squint at each possibility to see if the features are clear. You may need to **Edit** > **Undo Posterize** and return to the histogram levels several times to adjust the contrast before you find the best posterization.

12. Use the slider to get the right effect, or enter the number of levels you want. In this case, we have chosen 5 levels, which means five values will be used to compose this face. Notice there is detail, and the values are distributed evenly around the face.

First Image, step 12

Note: If you squint and still cannot achieve a result that looks realistic, you may need to undo all the posterizing (**Edit** > **Undo Posterize**) and make different changes to the histogram.

After undoing the posterizing, select  > **Levels** to view the histogram. Move the central arrow a little to the left or right.

Filter Cutout Alternative

There is an alternative way to fine-tune contrast using the **Filter Cutout**. The resulting portrait will appear a bit flattened and semi-abstract like an advertising billboard, which may be exactly what you are looking for. You do lose some control and some of the detail, especially around the eyes. Here are the steps:

1. Import photo and crop as desired.

2. Select **Enhance** > **Convert to Black and White**. (Since we are going the simpler route, just accept the **Portrait** option.)

3. From **Filters**, select **Artistic** and then select **Cutout**.

4. Try either 4 or 5 levels to see which works better.

Here is Danielle in 4 levels using the Filter Cutout.

Filter cutout result for First Image

Second Image

Here is a second image, which contains areas that are too light (overexposed), such as the background and the subject's hat. To correct this, you will need to balance the contrast better. We will begin with a cropped version of this image.

1. Elements offers three modes: Quick, Guided, and Expert. Using **Expert** mode, select the image.

Second Image, step 1

2. Select **Layer** > **Duplicate Layer**. Now your original image is part of the history and you can refer back to it as you work.

3. If needed, crop the image so your subject appears as you want it to be in your quilt.

Desaturating to Black & White

4. Select **Enhance** > **Convert to Black and White** to desaturate the image.

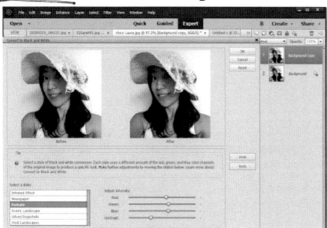

Second Image, step 4

View the black & white styles. Click on each style until you select the one with the highest contrast. We chose **Portraits**. Click **OK**.

5. Select ⟨🔍⟩ > **Levels** to view the histogram for this image. Notice the shape of the graph. It is fairly flat and only peaks on the right. This indicates there is not much contrast in this image and that it tends toward the lighter values. In fact it flattens out against the right wall, indicating that the highlights in this photo have been overexposed, or "blown out."

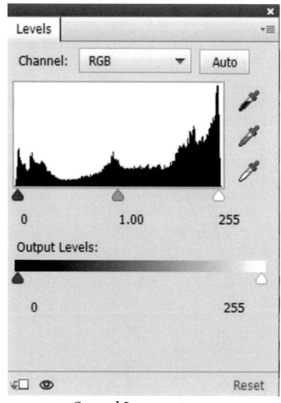

Second Image, step 5

Posterizing

6. Select ⟨🔍⟩ > **Posterize**. Choose **4** levels. Press **Enter**.

This is the result.

Second Image, step 6

The girl's hat is disappearing into the background, and it looks like she has a black eye on the right. Also the only light areas on her face are two white spots on her nose and tooth. Squinting does not help to provide a very good depiction of this face.

7. Raise the tonal levels to **5**. Press **Enter**.

Second Image, step 7

The eye area is improved, but she appears to have a medium-dark band across her eyes and cheek on the right side.

8. Undo the posterizing effects by selecting **Edit > Undo Modify Posterizing Layers**. You will need to repeat this undo until the image appears as the original desatured version.

9. Select ⊘ > **Levels** to return to the histogram. Center the middle peak by moving the middle arrow to **112**. Press **Enter**.

10. Select ⊘ > **Posterize** and posterize to **4** levels. Press **Enter**.

Second Image, step 10

The eye area is better, but there isn't much detail on her face, and there are still two white spots.

Tip: Shortcut Hint for steps 8-10. Instead of **Undo Posterize**, you can click on the Levels layer in History and move the center triangle right and left until the posterized pattern looks good.

11. Select  > **Posterize** and posterize to **5 levels. Press Enter**.

Second Image, step 11

This result is acceptable. The values seem better blended. You can see both eyes. Her nose looks like the right shape. There is a little more definition around her hat.

Filter Cutout Alternative

Again, here is the version using the Filter Cutout at 5 levels.

Filter cutout result for Second Image

Third Image

The background in the third image is very light compared with the subjects. There is too much contrast between the subjects and the background, which means the program will compress the values in the faces together, rather than enabling us to separate the values in the faces themselves. In this case, removing the background (isolating the faces from the background) and using the paintbrush tool to surround the figures in medium gray will solve this problem. We can later place the figures in a different background after we have posterized them.

Additionally, having two figures that are not equal in value range makes the process more complicated. In this case you may want to manipulate the photo twice and deal with each figure separately. We were able to balance them together, but working on each subject separately is definitely an option.

1. Select the image, using **Expert** mode.

Third Image, step 1

2. Select **Layer** > **Duplicate Layer**. Now your original image is part of the history and you can refer back to it as you work.

3. Crop the image to hone in on the subjects. Notice the background is very light and the subjects are dark. This is not a great recipe for this technique.

Removing the Background

4. Select the figures and then fill in the background with a color that is innocuous, like 50% gray.

5. Select 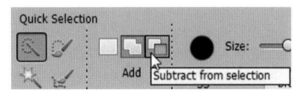 **Quick Selection Tool** from the toolbar on the left side of the elements window. You can adjust the brush size at the bottom of the window.

6. Select the background by carefully tracing the figures. If you grab too much or too little, you can adjust the selection with the **Add** and **Subtract** buttons at the bottom of the Elements window.

Third Image, step 6

7. Once the background is traced, select **Edit > Fill Selection**. Choose **50% gray**. Now the background will not define the overall contrast of the image. We can focus on the subjects.

Third Image, step 7

Result, Third Image, step 7

Tip: To remove the "marching ants" (dashed lines around the selected figures), press **Ctrl+D** or **ESC**. (On a macOS, use **Command+D**.)

The next challenge with this image is that the male subject is much lighter than the female. We will need to address this by either posterizing them separately or blending their values better.

Desaturating to Black & White

8. Select **Enhance > Convert to Black and White** to desaturate the image.

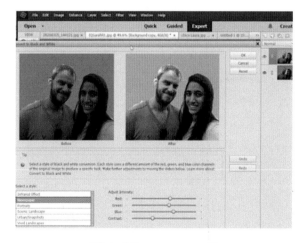

Third Image, step 8

9. Try each style until you find the most blended, pleasing version. We chose **Newspaper**. Click **OK**.

Third Image, step 9

10. Select 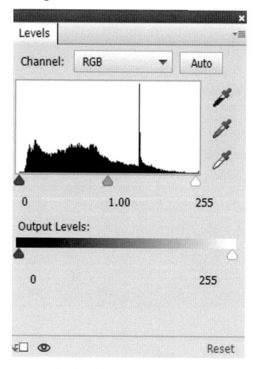 > **Levels** to view the histogram for this image.

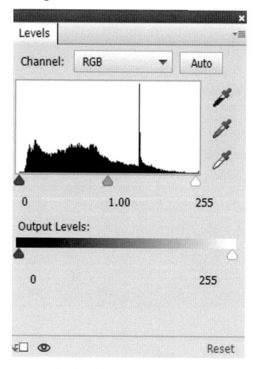

Third Image, step 10

Note: The middle arrow is under the mid-values rather than the tall peak.

Posterize

11. Select ⬭ > **Posterize**. Choose level **4**. Press **Enter**. This is the result.

Third Image, step 11

Notice the strange mustache and the dark neck on the male figure at level 4. The female has large patches on her face, and the values are not well blended.

12. Posterize to level **5**.

Third Image, step 12

34

In this result the male posterization looks reasonable. The female has very little definition and she has dark patches around her eyes. Let's go back to the histogram and make some adjustments. (**Edit** > **Undo**)

13. Adjust the arrows to blend the overall contrast. Move the arrow on the right from 255 to **223**, which is where the graph starts to rise on the right side. The center arrow is at 1.00 already. Press **Enter**. (See histogram in Step 10 for reference.)

14. Posterize to level **4**. Press **Enter**.

Third Image, step 14

Notice how the male's head has disappeared on the left side because it is overexposed. His neck is undefined and very dark. The darkest values on the female's face don't look right. Let's see the results of posterizing to 5 levels.

15. Posterize to level **5**. Press **Enter**.

Third Image, step 15

This time the result is very good. The blending in both faces is fairly gradual, so you will not get a patchy outcome. The darkest shadows and lightest areas look realistic when we squint.

Filter Cutout Alternative

As an alternative we again show you the result using the quickie Filter Cutout style in 5 levels.

Filter cutout result for Third Image

More Examples and Tips

Of course if you start out with a good photo you have a lot less work to do. Here is an example.

This was easily cropped to faces only, because the background adds little to the story. The photo was simple to desaturate and posterize into a nice balance of values. By cropping in, we emphasize the bond between the subjects.

Here is the posterized version.

This next image of an older face has a few problems. In Chapter 6 when we explain how to cut out the pattern, this will become clearer. However, we do want to mention a few points regarding the posterized result now.

In this pattern, because of the angle of the camera, the subject's prominent nose produces a very dark shadow on her lower lip. This cast shadow should be downplayed here so it will not appear as if she has a hole in her lip.

In other words, we are not slaves to the posterization values. We can adapt the values in the posterized result, so the effect is more pleasing to the eye.

Another challenge arises when we try to use old, low-resolution vintage photos, which we really want to make into quilts for sentimental reasons. When students send these to create patterns, we groan a little. In this example, Shlomit Katz wanted to make a quilt in memory of her grandparents who perished in the Holocaust.

After a lot of trial and error, the resulting, really pixelated pattern is good enough to make a portrait, although it won't have a lot of detail. If that's acceptable, and sometimes even true to an old blurry image, then it's worth using. Here's an example of the photo after posterizing to 5 levels.

Tip: If you want, you can print the image on full-sized labels rather than printing on paper and then using spray adhesive, as explained in Chapter 6. Then you just remove the paper backing from the label, and stick the label to the right side of the fabrics. Make sure the labels are "repositionable," so the pattern does not stick to the front of your work permanently! You can print enlarged images on these labels by sticking them together in rows as we discussed previously.

Tip: For those of you in the U.S., if you prefer enlarging and printing your photo using a commercial program other than Elements, refer to:

- Blockposters.com
- Posterazor.sourceforge.io
- Rapidresizer.com
- Rasterbator.net

Alternatively, you can also send your image to a commercial printer (like Office Max or Office Depot) with instructions about your desired, full-size image.

5 Values in Fabrics

We return here to the concept of value, and how it relates to fabric.

As we have said, value (shading and highlighting) give form to two-dimensional objects, so they appear to have volume. An orange suddenly looks round on a two-dimensional surface when you add shading and light. How do we apply value theories to fabric choices? How do we use fabric choices to illustrate light shining on a face?

There are a number of aspects of color to define here, because the qualities of color you choose set the stage:

- **Hues** are the pure colors in the color wheel.
- **Tones** are pure colors mixed with gray.
- **Shades** are pure colors mixed with black.
- **Tints** are pure colors mixed with white (what we sometimes refer to as **pastels**).

Tints or pastels hint at innocence; toned colors whisper quiet or calm; shades create drama; and the intensity of the hues suggests excitement and helps create the emotional effect desired.

Using a range of light to dark (i.e. a range of values) gradually takes the viewer from shadow into the light and provides depth.

Sorting Values

Let's try a short exercise. Pick a hue from your fabric stash. Let's choose blue for example. Pull out 5–6 examples of blue fabrics that range from very light to very dark. Line them up on a surface. Arrange the fabrics to make sure the values gradually change from light to dark, squinting as you go. Take a photo of this lineup of fabrics. Look at the photo beginning with the light end. Is each value distinct? Do the values gradually darken until they end in very dark?

There are tools you can use to check your value choices, called value finders, which are red (ruby value finders) and green filters. When you look through them, you can distinguish the light, medium, and dark qualities of the fabrics. You can tell if any of the midtones are too alike, and you can make sure the fabrics are arranged in the correct order.

Another trick to see differences in value is to look at the fabrics as a black & white image. Desaturate the photo you took previously, so it is black & white. Now look at the comparison of values to be sure they are in the right order and that none of the fabrics are the same value.

This process will get easier after you repeat it a few times. Meanwhile, after studying your lineup, make any adjustments until you are satisfied with the collection.

When you look at a portrait, you can see there are different values in the skin. Technically speaking these are the levels that result in values:

- **Lights** (brightest stage)
- **Halftones** or midtones, which transition lights to shadows
- **Shadows**
- **Reflected light**
- **Cast shadows**, which are created when the subject blocks the light (darkest stage)

By posterizing a photo after desaturating it to black & white, the computer detects these value differences and assigns values from white to black to each area. By posterizing to five levels you simulate five levels of distinct values. It's your job to find fabrics to represent these posterized values, maintaining the distinctness as well as blending the tones.

The lightest value should be nearly white, preferably with a glow, to simulate light. The darkest value should be nearly black to offer the greatest contrast. Dark recedes. Light advances. The mid-tone values should also progress from lighter to darker. They must be distinct enough so you can see a value change if you set these fabrics side by side. If there is a question about whether the values are sufficiently distinct at the lighter end vs. the darker end, try making your lighter values only slightly darker than your "white" value, and be sure that only the very darkest value is truly dark.

Ok, let's get started.

As an example, we again used this image of Danielle, which we posterized to five layers and then desaturated.

Working the Blues

Here is a lineup of blue fabrics, ordered from light to dark. Squint. Would you change any of these fabrics? Look at the desaturated version of the lineup. Are the values distinct enough?

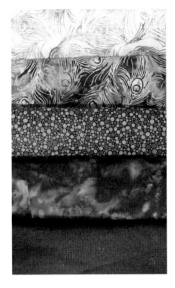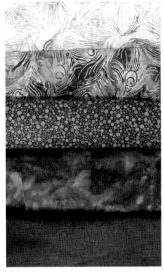

And here is the quilt...

"Danielle - Blue Tones," Cindy

Can you tell what is wrong with this result?

If you look at the black & white version of the lineup of fabrics, you can see more easily that the 2nd value jumps too far from the very lightest. The 3rd and 4th values are actually too close. The top of her face looks fine. She has volume and depth, but from her cheeks down to her chin and neck, the values are too dark. You can definitely make out her likeness to the original, but the fabric choices detract from the overall result. The dotted, dominant fabric in the middle is too dark, which detracts from the final result. It is harder to use a fabric that has widely varying values as this fabric does.

Tip: All is not lost if your end product is too dark. When quilting, use lighter thread in the areas you want to lighten. This will go a long way in "repairing" and reversing dark fabric choices that are not that successful.

Adding Some Gold

Let's look at another set of fabrics with more distinct value changes.

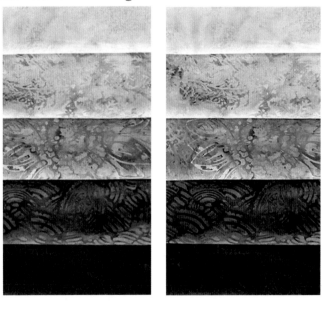

Here is the result of using them in the same portrait.

"Danielle - Golden Tones," Cindy

This quilt is much more successful than the previous darker-valued version. You can easily see the likeness of the subject. The values blend well and do not compete with each other. This is an overall harmonious result.

We intentionally started here by showing you a portrait made with unconventional colors and patterns. Really, as long as you capture a person's likeness and the twinkle in the eye, you can use any combination of colors and prints. Phyllis's mantra: "Believable is more important than realistic."

Skin Tones

You can of course work with more predictable, traditional fabrics, which means working with the range of colors associated with skin tones, but that opens a whole other "can of worms"... (Here we are using the word tone in a colloquial way, as it refers to the mix of colors in the skin of any particular individual.)

What if you want to reproduce the exact skin colors? Here's what you do: Cut out a 2" square of thick white paper, and punch out a hole the size of your fingernail in the center. Move it around your subject's skin, and notice the actual color showing through the hole. At each spot you check, the color will be slightly different. Oil painters reproduce skin color by subtly changing the mix of paint on their palette. It is a lot more challenging to do this in fabric.

There are many factors that affect skin tones, including ambient temperature, color of the light shining on the subject, amount of time in the sun, etc.

Supposing you mix paints to achieve skin tones. How much yellow is in skin color? How much red? How much blue? Is your subject's skin warmer (redder) or cooler (bluer)?

Where does your subject come from? Ethnicity definitely influences skin color, as well as hair color and individual genetic mix. Every subject has a unique range of values and colors.

Finally, is skin actually pink for anyone or is it more peach-toned? The general consensus is, there are no "normal" skin tones. Oil painters try to match what they observe under the light that they choose. In this oil painting by Phyllis, notice the range of skin colors.

"The Purple Hat," Phyllis

The technique in the resulting quilt is less accurate than the method used for the quilts done with the blue and golden toned fabrics. Although conventional tones were used, this technique required a lot more attention to reach a result that resembled the subject.

Here is the quilt.

"Danielle - Skin Tones," Cindy

Easy enough for an oil painter, who can make slight alterations in hue and value with a little addition of one color to another. To do the same thing in fabric, we use many different fabrics and threads to match and blend all the slight variations in just one face.

Here is one more version of Danielle. This line-up of fabrics with more "typical" skin tones was used for a slightly different layered technique, which was based on "eyeing" the values.

Notice the "band-aid" effect, because the fabrics are nearly solid and therefore do not blend as well as the prints, that is, unless you posterize to 10 levels. Once quilted, this effect lessens, resulting in a more realistic portrait.

Unfortunately we have all seen the unnatural effect that occurs if the quilting lines simply follow the edges of the patches, worsening the "band-aid" effect. That's why Chapter 7 will explain how contour quilting solves that problem.

Wild Fabrics

In earlier chapters we discussed the need to ensure contrast between hard edges (eyes vs. face, for example) and soft edges (the subtle change of values in the curve of the cheek, where we don't want to see harsh lines in a realistic portrait). One way to create soft edges is with the use of layers of tulle and stitching. Highlighting can be added with light, bright fabrics, such as shiny, bright organzas.

Another good way to mask the dividing lines between fabric values is to use prints that contain a variety of colors. The print chosen for each level should have a similar value throughout the fabric. Slight variations in design and internal values between adjacent fabrics will smooth out the gradation and also add some excitement to the portrait. Thus, we can make portraits with very unrealistic fabrics that still completely capture a likeness and are quite believable, as long as we follow the value guidelines. You just have to trust the process!

Consider these arrays of printed fabrics arranged according to value.

"My Lively Granddaughters," Phyllis

Stitching also plays a role in blending, but it's important to remember that unless the fabric values are chosen correctly, the thread will not be able to compensate. The value of the fabric will be the dominant player (unless the quilting is so tight that it obscures the underlying fabric, as in a technique called thread painting).

Here is a self-portrait by Phyllis's student, Christy. The decision to make a portrait from either mild or wild fabrics affects the entire mood of the portrait, but not its believability!

Here are four quilts portraying printed fabrics of different values that blend into each other.

"Self Portrait," Christy Hoffmann

44

6 Collaged Portraits

Why Layers?

Prior to today's digital printing process, printing required multiple passes through a press, with each progressive layer adding a darker value. The idea of layering colors in printing was the inspiration for layering values of fabric.

To transfer the image to fabric, we will introduce three processes:

- **Layered** collage technique
- **Scrappy** collage technique
- **Combination** of both techniques

At the end of this chapter, we will mention alternative methods of transferring images to fabric.

Then we'll discuss how to quilt the portraits to enhance the realistic effect. Of course you can always add on more collage, surface design, embroidery, or thread painting.

Layered Collage Technique

In the layered collage technique, instead of using small bits of fabric, full fabric sheets of progressively darker layers are cut up to reveal the lighter layers below.

Make sure you have a full-size color version of your photo to refer to as you work. Sometimes it is hard to distinguish small details, and it is really important to have the original image on hand.

Here is the process with each step illustrated.

Read through the entire process once before you begin working to familiarize yourself with the steps.

Reference photo for Layered Collage "Jeanne"

We will hone in on Jeanne's face.

Reference close-up for Layered Collage

This photo was posterized to four levels. We first chose the fabrics in a progression of light to dark, as we discussed in Chapter 5. The number of fabrics is equal to the number of levels in the posterized pattern. Here we have four levels and four fabrics. The lightest light is #1. The next darker fabrics are #2 followed by #3. The darkest dark is #4.

45

1. Make sure you have one copy of the pattern for each posterized level (value). In this case you have four levels, so you need **4 copies of the pattern**. You will be attaching a pattern to each fabric, beginning with #2. Set aside one copy for reference.

Note: Fabric #1 is the backing fabric for the portrait. It will not be cut up and therefore does not require a pattern.

Set the patterns aside for now.

2. We will be working with fabrics cut to the size of a pattern. Cut one piece of fabric for each posterized level (value). Your lightest light should be very pale and your darkest dark may even be black.

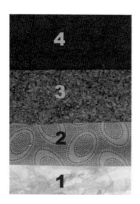 

Layered Collage, step 2

3. Apply Mistyfuse® fusible web to the **back** of each of the fabrics, except for the lightest value (#1). You don't want Mistyfuse on the back of fabric #1, or you could mistakenly fuse #1 to your ironing board while you are working!

Tip: Mistyfuse is our recommended choice of fusible web when working with multiple layers, because it is very thin, lightweight, flexible and does not change the feel of the fabric. You can use a different lightweight fusible web instead. Heavier fusible products will produce a very stiff end result that is difficult to stitch through, because there are so many layers.
In addition, there is no added benefit to having backing paper on the fusible web for this technique. In fact, if you use a fusible with paper backing, **remove the paper before you do any cutting.**

4. We use repositionable spray adhesive to temporarily adhere the paper patterns to the **front** side (right side) of the fabric.
Apply the spray adhesive to the front side of fabrics #2, #3, and #4, which you previously prepared with Mistyfuse.

Tip: We recommend Odif 505® Temporary Adhesive spray found in craft and fabric stores. Brands like Sullivans™ and Easy-Tack™ work well. As long as the can says "temporary" or "repositionable" it should work fine.

5. Next, stick a pattern sheet to the adhesive applied to the **front** side of each fabric (#2, #3, and #4). Number each fabric set accordingly on the upper right corner of the paper pattern.

Here we see the original photo in black & white; the three fabric sheets with the posterized pattern affixed to the right side of fabric sheets #2, #3, and #4; and a can of repositionable adhesive spray.

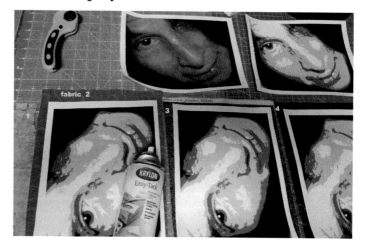

Layered Collage, step 5

By the end of the project, this is the order of the fused layers you will prepare.

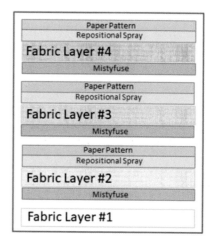

6. Trim the three fabric sets—fabric and pattern layers — for #2, #3, and #4 to the outer edges of the image, so they are all **exactly** the same size. Use the corners as registration marks to ensure that each layer is exactly lined up with the previous layer. They will be placed on top of each other later.

7. Number all the values on the paper pattern that you adhered to fabric #2. This will give you an understanding of the complexity of your design.

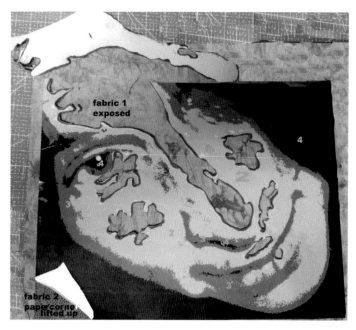

Layered Collage, step 10

11. Remove the pattern paper from the two fused layers (#1 and #2).

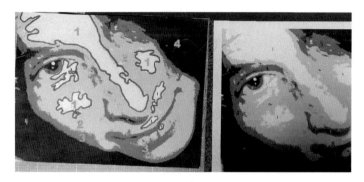

Layered Collage, step 7

8. Begin by assigning #1 to the lightest value. Circle all the #1 values in the pattern (all the lightest posterized areas) with a colored pen or pencil.

9. Cut out all the #1 circled areas from the #2 pattern/fabric set you are working on.

Note: You may need these discarded fabrics later, so keep them on hand and intact.

10. Place fabric #2, which is still connected to the pattern, directly on fabric #1. Fuse fabric #2 to fabric #1 by ironing the layers.

Tip: Use a silicon sheet or parchment paper while ironing to protect your iron and ironing board cover.

In this photo the lightest pieces (#1s) were cut out from the #2 layer. Fabric #2 has been fused to fabric #1. We now see the lightest value fabric (#1) peeking through the cut away openings in fabric #2.

Layered Collage, step 11

12. On the pattern sheet adhered to fabric #3, which is the next darker fabric, circle value #1s and #2s with a different colored pen or pencil.

47

13. From layer #3, cut out all the #1 and #2 circled areas, either together or separately, depending on whether or not they are contiguous in the pattern. Set the contiguous #1 and #2 pieces on the side to be used next.

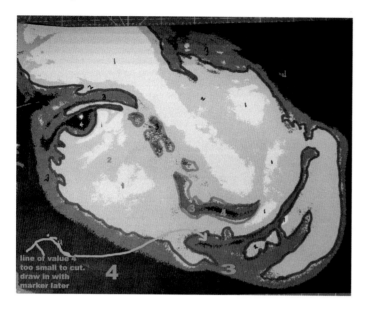

Layered Collage, step 13

Note: In this photo, the large, contiguous #1 and #2 areas that were just cut out are outlined in **red**. Within the **red** area are some "islands" of levels #3 and #4 outlined in green. The large #1 and #2 pieces you set aside will serve as a "template" for placement of the green outlined areas (#3s and #4s).

14. Place the remaining outer frame from layer #3 on top of the fused #1 and #2 layers. Make sure to match corners carefully so all the layers line up. Iron layer #3 to the fused #1 and #2 layers. Remove the paper pattern from layer #3.

Layered Collage, step 14

15. From the contiguous, intact #1 and #2 pieces that you saved in step 13, cut out the #3 green islands. Set them aside.

Note: Regarding cutting, don't bother with tiny dots of different values here and there unless they define the eyes, nostrils, etc. Wrinkles at the corners of eyes or other very thin lines would be too thin if they were cut out from fabric. It is better to add these details with quilting. Generally, don't try to cut pieces thinner than a few threads wide.

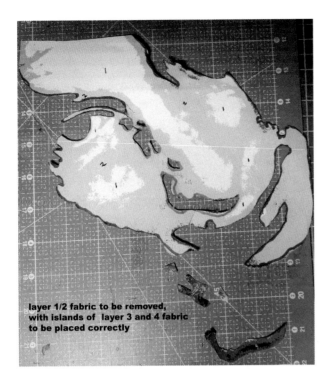

Layered Collage, step 15

16. Take the fabric-backed pattern (contiguous, intact #1 and #2) from which you just cut out the green islands in Step 15. Remove the fabric. Keep the paper. Place only the paper on fused layers #1 and #2.
Because this pattern piece was cut from these layers, the paper pattern will fit exactly, like a jigsaw puzzle.

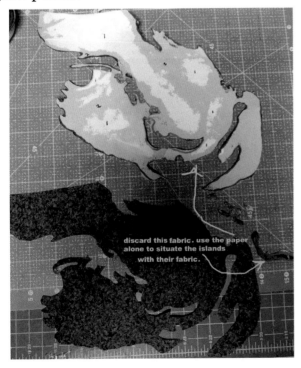

Layered Collage, step 16

Note: We tell you to detach the fabric from the paper pattern at this stage, so you don't fuse unwanted fabric to your layers.

17. Fit the green island pieces into the holes in the paper pattern. Tap them down with an iron so they will stay in place. When they are all in place fuse them down and remove the paper pattern from each green island piece.

This photo shows the first three layers fused together. Notice the added intermediate values, as well as white and black lines added to this photo.

Layered Collage, step 17

By the time you get to layer #4 (or #5 or even more in some cases), the areas to be saved will be widely spaced without connections between them. By using intact pattern pieces, you can place the darker value pieces in their exact locations.

Tip: If the original photo is low resolution the pixels may be more pronounced. You can cut smooth edges rather than following the square shapes of the pixels.

18. When all layers are ironed in place, the quilt will resemble the posterized pattern, with appropriate values filling intended areas. Check to make sure all values are in their correct positions in case a piece was left out somewhere or added inadvertently. Correct as needed.

19. Look at the fused, layered quilt. Now is the time to add white ink for eye catchlights, black ink where the level #4 lines were too thin to cut, and little pieces of similar or intermediate values to delineate the features a bit more.

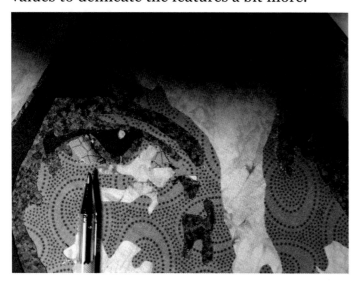

Layered Collage, step 19

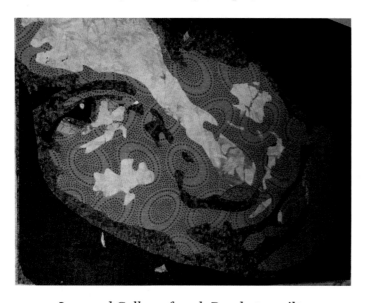

Layered Collage fused. Ready to quilt.

20. You can now cut out the portrait and fuse it to another background area as desired. The next step is quilting the portrait in Chapter 7.

Note: The described process was from light to dark. As an alternative, you can also work from dark to light. We usually work light to dark to avoid dark fabrics showing through light areas, but if you want the dark values to appear under the lighter values, reverse the process just described. Once it's quilted, whichever layer is on top usually won't matter.

Another Example of Layered Collage Technique

Fabric portraits based on photos of babies are challenging because the contrast on their faces is too low. When we try to break these faces down in layers, it is difficult not to make them look hard. It can, however, be done! You will probably need a lot more than four layers to accomplish this. This quilt of a "Peeper" required 10 layers.

"Peeper," Phyllis

Scrappy Collage Technique

For those of you who have done paper collage, this will seem familiar. We can start from a drawing with shading, as in a pencil drawing, or we can start by creating a posterized pattern, akin to the layered collage technique.

Read the entire procedure before beginning.

We'll start with this photo of Dan.

Print one copy of the drawing for reference as well as a posterized pattern of the drawing. Both copies should be the full size of the intended finished portrait.

Reference photo for "Scrappy Dan"

In this example the photo was posterized to four layers.

Posterized reference photo for "Scrappy Dan"

1. On the posterized copy, mark the values using #1, #2, #3, and #4, going from light to dark.

2. Cut a piece of Lite Steam-A-Seam 2® to the same size as the drawing.

Tip: We will describe this process using our preferred choice, Warm Company's Lite Steam-A-Seam 2®, which is a pressure-sensitive fusible webbing with paper on both sides. It is especially suited to this technique, because once you peel the top paper off, you can temporarily stick fabric pieces to the sticky web until they are heat-fused. You leave the back paper attached until you are ready to permanently fuse the glue layer to your backing fabric.

Depending on where you live, fusible web product options will vary with paper on both sides or just one side. These options will also work well: Pellon® EZ-Steam® II, Quilters Select™ Appli-Stick by Floriani, or E-Zee Cut® Appliqué Magic by Madeira. Make sure whatever you choose says the webbing is "pressure sensitive," which means you will be able to lift and move fabrics until they are heat-fused. We leave the choice to you.

3. Using a lightbox or window, trace the pattern with a fine, permanent black marker onto the front paper of the Lite Steam-A-Seam 2, so the yellow gridded, paper side is down.

Tip: If you are using a webbing without paper on both sides, trace the reversed image directly on the back of the webbing, and then flip it over before you start adhering fabric to the sticky side. You should see the image with the correct orientation through the glue layer.

4. Set aside the posterized pattern. Flip the Lite Steam-A-Seam 2 over so the faintly gridded side is on top, and use the same marker to retrace the pattern on the yellow gridded back paper. The pattern will now be the reverse image. For reference, you can add the value numbers to this back-side reversed pattern.

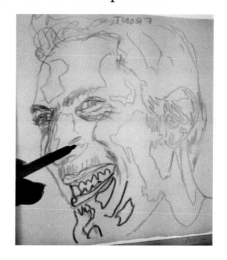

Scrappy Collage, step 4

5. Prepare the fabrics by dividing your stash of printed fabrics into piles according to value. The number of fabric piles is equal to the number of levels in the posterized pattern. Here we have four values and four fabric piles. The lightest light is #1. The next darker fabrics are #2, followed by #3. The darkest dark is #4. Use several prints in each value. You don't need large amounts of each fabric.

6. Use your rotary cutter to slash the fabrics into randomly-shaped small pieces, about 1-2", which you can reshape and resize as needed.

Scrappy Collage, step 6

7. Flip the Lite Steam-A-Seam 2 again so the top paper is on top. Peel off the top layer of paper, and set it aside for later. The sticky glue webbing will now be exposed. The backing paper will be on the bottom, and the orientation of the drawing that shows through the glue webbing will be correct.

8. Now start to fill in the various value-designated areas with the appropriate value scraps. They will adhere to the sticky base. Do not worry if the scraps overlap each other a little as long as some part of the scrap touches the base. Do not leave gaps between scraps.

Here the pattern is partly filled in. Notice the size of the fabric pieces.

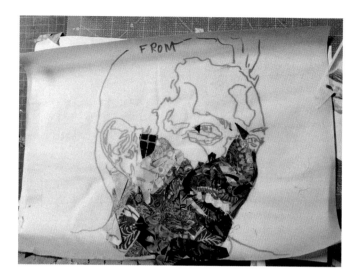

Scrappy Collage, step 8

9. When you reach the edges of each feature, such as the eyes and nose, trim the scraps with scissors to fit within the pattern lines. Notice if the value section is angled upward or downward or gets thicker or thinner, and trim the pieces to roughly accommodate the shape. Keep referring to the posterized pattern and the original photo to guide you.

10. Check to see if a scrap looks too light or too dark or doesn't define the features as well as you would like. The pieces are attached only temporarily and can be adjusted easily until you are happy with them all.

11. Continue to fill in all the sections until you are satisfied with the overall effect. It helps to squint and to take photos at various points to see if your collage reflects the drawing.

12. When you are happy with the result, take it to the ironing board, cover it with the original front paper layer, and steam iron it.

Scrappy Collage, step 12

13. Once the pieces are fused together, cut the face out from the surrounding Lite Steam-A-Seam 2. Then carefully remove the paper from the front and the back of the webbing.

14. You are now ready to fuse the collaged portrait onto the background of your choice. Place the collage on the background, cover it with parchment paper or a non-stick ironing sheet, like a silicon sheet, and steam iron it. Steam it very thoroughly. You want to really melt the glue, otherwise it will make your needle sticky when you quilt it.

15. Decorate the background with any collaged or fusible-backed embellishments you want to add. When the entire scene is complete, cover it with dark tulle. Audition different colors of dark tulle. Black always works, but dark purple, dark brown or navy blue may be more pleasing.

Tip: Do not use light tulle unless you want your portrait to be in a cloud of smoke or a thick fog.

16. Layer the backing, batting, fused top and tulle. Spray baste or pin (unless you are going to quilt it on a longarm) all the layers and take them to the sewing machine.

Note: Do not iron directly on the tulle. It will melt.

Scrappy Collage, step 13

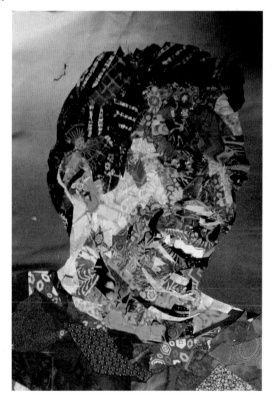

Scrappy Collage fused. Ready to quilt, step 16

The final quilted version of this scrappy collage appears in Chapter 7.

Other Examples of Scrappy Collage Technique

"Hula Kane" is another portrait done in the scrappy style. The posterized version is followed by the unquilted collage. The portrait is ready for tulle and quilting.

This is another example of a collaged face by Rita Gazubey.

"Portrait of Lyuba," Rita Gazubey

Posterized photo for "Hula Kane"

Meriul Easton captured her great-grandson in this engaging collaged quilt. The quilting lines follow the contours of his face.

Unquilted, "Hula Kane," Phyllis

"Life Is Good," Meriul Easton

Combined Techniques

When it is necessary to posterize too many layers, it's easier to see the posterized layers in color. Here is an example of a partial face, broken down into 12 layers from "Lovebirds Two," by Phyllis.

Here is the partially-layered collage of the face from "Lovebirds Two."

Here is the collage of the face from "Lovebirds Two," ready for quilting.

We saw the reference photo, completed collage and completed quilt on pp 11–12. Now you can see how we arrived at the final result.

This detail of a face of Moses was done in the blended style as well. The full quilt, "Early Tablets," by Phyllis appears on p 84.

Alternative Methods: Image to Fabric

There are other methods to transfer an image to fabric that require practice. You can create a pattern by training your eye to separate values.

Alternatively, there are teachers who instruct you to simply enlarge a good contrast photograph, and then trace or outline both the facial features and the perceived value changes.

To create a portrait, you can paint, draw, embroider, or otherwise treat your fabric like a support (typically paper, canvas, wood, etc.). Then you can choose from an endless variety of media, such as colored pencils, inks, thickened dyes, acrylic paints, oil sticks, watercolors, and crayons to embellish the work.

"Off to Market" is an example of a portrait painted on fabric with acrylic paints and then quilted. It could have been painted on canvas, which is stiffer fabric, but it is the quilting that makes this a fabric portrait.

"Off to Market," Phyllis

Some artists print their photos directly onto fabric. Sherry Davis Kleinman digitally manipulated a portrait of her granddaughter on her iPad, printed it on fabric, and then heavily thread painted it by hand and machine.

"A Moment in Time with Genevieve,"
Sherry Davis Kleinman

Kathleen Kastles puts the whole process back on its ear. She painted this whole-cloth quilted face to look like it is made of patches of fabric.

"Pensive," Kathleen Kastles
Photo Credit: José Morales,
Xinia Productions, Maui, HI

Basically, we are telling you there is no end to the many possible techniques available. There are other printing techniques: batik, pastels, colored pencils. There are endless ways artists transfer their images to fabric. We encourage you to use every trick you can. Our motto is,

"Whatever works!"

It's All About the Face (https://www.faccbook.com/groups/itsallabouttheface), the Facebook group associated with this book will show you many examples of painted, printed, and embroidered portraits in different settings, backgrounds, and compositions.

Book Two will delve into all these methods of creating portraits from painting to printing, as well as using different methods, genres, styles and media in far greater detail.

7 Contour Quilting

Hundreds of students ask, "I love my portrait, but how do I quilt it so I don't ruin the realistic effect?" Or we hear, "I was afraid to sew any lines in the face, so I left it unquilted. When I got to the show where it was hung, I noticed a big fat wrinkle across the whole face."

We feel strongly that:

Yes, you can quilt it.
&
Yes, you should quilt it.

It will definitely enhance the realistic effect.

Functionally, quilting connects the three layers of a quilt—top, batting and back—but that is just one aspect of quilting. In this chapter, as promised, we will discuss how to bring our portraits to life using thread.

Just a couple of **notes** before we begin quilting:
- You will be working on a quilt sandwich consisting of a top, batting, and a back. If you use stabilizer between the top and the batting, it will help keep the quilt flat while you are quilting it, particularly on a domestic machine.
- Please don't use puffy batting for your portrait, unless you really want to accentuate the wrinkles. Cotton, dense battings, and even flatter filling material will give you a smoother-looking face.

Free Motion Quilting

Imagine, as we describe the quilting process, that our needle is drawing with thread on our quilt, like a pencil on paper. The technique for this process is called Free Motion Quilting (FMQ), which can be done on a domestic machine or a long arm.

Domestic Machine

FMQ on a domestic machine is done when the "feed dogs" are down, so the machine doesn't pull your fabric as you sew. (Check your machine manual for how to lower the feed dogs.) Instead, you move the quilt with your hands in any direction that you want while the needle moves up and down. Most quilters also use special "free motion" or "darning" feet on their machines, so the fabric glides smoothly under the feet without drag on the fabric.

There are tacky substances, like sortKwik® or Lickity GRIP®, to aid in traction, so your hands don't slip as you move the fabric. You can also find special gloves or rings to hold the fabric, but they are cumbersome.

Some sewing machines have built-in stitch regulators. This means once you start sewing, the machine identifies and maintains the same stitch length until you stop sewing. On machines without this feature, you need to control the stitch length yourself by moving the fabric slowly or quickly with your hands while your foot is on the pedal. If you maintain a constant speed on the pedal, the faster you move the fabric, the larger the stitches will be. Conversely, the slower you move the fabric, the smaller the stitches.

The size of the needle depends on how thick your thread is, but generally on a domestic machine, a size 90/14 is a good choice.

The hole in a "topstitch" needle is larger and easier to thread. Topstitch needles are also strong enough to carry the thread through several layers of fused fabric. Microtex needles are also commonly used for quilting multiple layers of tightly woven fabrics, because they help prevent skipped stitches.

Long Arm Machine

On a long arm machine, you actually move the needle over the stationary quilt that is mounted on a frame. So it's more like moving a pencil over a stationary piece of paper. Most long arm quilters also use special "free motion" or "darning" feet on their machines, so the feet glide smoothly over the fabric. Typically size 16 or 18 sharp needles work best for quilting many layers on long arms. If you want smaller holes, use a size 12 or 14 needle. Most long arms have stitch regulation that maintain a constant stitch length.

Thread

If your piece is created from skin-toned fabrics, you will probably select skin-toned threads. Match the value of the thread in each area to the value of the underlying fabric. We usually use the matching color for each area in monochromatic portraits and value-adjusted variegated thread for the wild prints. But as we have said, non-realistic can also be believable, and then your thread can be any color.

We recommend that only those of you who are comfortable with FMQ use contrasting thread, which can be distracting if it is not quilted smoothly. Otherwise, match your thread to the fabrics on top.

We choose thread according to color, rather than focusing on the type of thread. If the facial fabric is shiny, we might use polyester or rayon threads, because both of these are vibrant, shiny options. If the background has a matte finish, cotton thread will blend well, because it also has a matte finish.

We are sewing so many lines of quilting on an art quilt, there is little concern for the strength of fibers. Consequently, rayon thread, though a weaker fiber than cotton or polyester, has a place in fiber design. However, it is important to make sure you are not using old or cheap thread, which will break and frustrate you while you are sewing. Stick to name brand, quality threads like Superior Threads®, Wonderfil®, YLI, Aurifil™, Gütermann, Madeira, and Sulky®.

General Tips

We assume that you are proficient at FMQ. If not, there are many instructional books or videos available.

Check your tension. It often helps to lower the top tension on your machine to prevent the bobbin thread from showing on the top.

In the bobbin you may also want to use the same color as the top thread. If you use fairly thin threads, like 60 weight, and busy prints on the back, you will be able to hide really irregular or jerky stitches.

Practice, practice, practice. Then you will be ready to consider how to design your stitching pattern.

Contour Quilting

If you were on a hike, you would follow the terrain on the trail. In much the same way, when representing anatomical features, such as faces or hands or feet, we follow the contours of the bones using contour lines.

From an art perspective, there are three types of contour lines:

- **Exterior contour lines**: Indicate shape like in coloring books or silhouettes. They are mainly outlines.
- **Interior contour lines**: Lines that sketch along the important interior shapes. These are usually used in painting as "blocking-in" lines that are meant to be erased.
- **Cross contour lines**: Parallel lines that follow the curvature of an object and indicate volume. They follow the shape: curve or straight, round or angular, up or down—changing direction as the shape dictates. Where features overlap, they stop at the edge. **These are our quilting lines.**

The direction of these curved contour lines and the degree of curvature is dependent on your point of view. If you look at a figure straight on, the middle contour lines will be straight. The lines above the midline will curve up, and the curves below the midline will curve down. If you look up at a figure the curves will all curve up. From above, the curves will curve down.

After studying many, many fabric portraits quilted in different ways, we have formed a strong, though not always popular, opinion. **We feel the main purpose of the quilting is to define the contours of the facial features.**

Blending Values

In Chapter 6 we discussed how the values are layered into a cohesive collage. We described the "islands" that had to be cut out and placed in exactly the right places to show where values changed. These value changes also correspond to where the contour lines change direction.

We are not interested in isolating the value changes by outlining these islands or patches, because we feel it ruins the portrait effect. Quilting around the edges of the patches, as though they are actual features, results in a loss of the 3D effect and creates weird lines that don't follow anatomy, wrinkles, features, or body curves. (See pp 72–73 in this chapter for additional explanation.)

By stitching over the patches and across the boundary between patches, we help blend all the values. If we were painting a classic portrait in oil, the goal would be to avoid hard edges and combine colors where one paint meets another. This goal is the same when using thread. We want to be sure to mix the values as we move from lighter to darker, and vice versa. By stitching back and forth across the junction of two different values of fabric, we soften the hard edges inherent in fabric junctions and blend the strands of thread. Always remember our goal is to produce a believable result.

"Lovebirds Three: Joy" is first shown unquilted. In the quilted version, notice how the quilting lines blend the edges and give the faces a harmonious and smoother appearance.

Unquilted collage, "Lovebirds Three: Joy," Phyllis

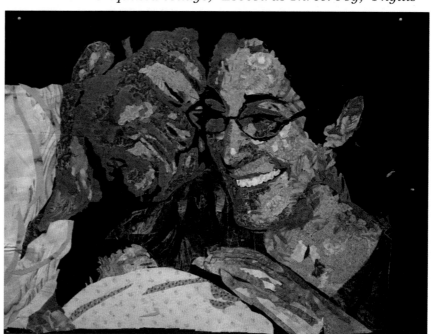

Quilted collage, "Lovebirds Three: Joy," Phyllis

Creating Volume

By following the contours of the face with cross contour lines, we can enhance the sense of volume we have achieved with the progressive values of our fabrics. We can intensify the shape so it is realistic and reflects the depth of the face, rather than a flat, distorted portrayal.

Again, let's compare quilting to drawing with thread. Sometimes we do not draw every line. Likewise, if we do not stitch every line, we still want the viewer to understand that volume exists. We hint at this recognition using partially stitched lines, thicker and thinner stitching, shading, value changes, etc. Typically we don't want to outline features, like eyes or a nose, because that does not further the illusion of volume, and frankly looks quite artificial.

If you change the direction of contour lines, you can build up the darker areas vs. lighter areas. This creates form without the need for outlining or drawing lines around features. For example, by varying the density of the quilting lines, we can make an area appear to recede.

Straight quilting lines across a face would flatten the features, so instead we use curved lines to accentuate the roundness and contours to create volume.

On the other hand, quilting lines can help us define the features when the posterized pattern doesn't separate them. For example, if the nose and cheek are the same value, only a change in direction of the quilting contour lines will distinguish them.

Guiding Lines

So, how do we know what lines to follow? When we look back at our study of anatomy, we notice that the parallel striations of the muscle fibers form the same cross contour lines as our quilting. The right side of this skeleton, which is covered with muscle striations, illustrates what we mean. If we overlaid our contour lines on this skeleton they would echo the muscles of the face and body, just like skin follows the grooves in the muscles.

There are areas where the bones are not covered by muscle or where soft tissue builds up in its own form, such as a nose or breast. Then we follow the resulting form. Likewise, when the subject is young and unwrinkled, the contour lines follow the bony hills and valleys. If we consider clothing in these terms, a clingy dress would be fitted over the underlying figure.

How to Plan Quilting Lines

We used this photo of Danielle earlier in the book. Now we are showing the map Cindy used to mark the contours of the bone structure of her face. These lines are like topographical lines showing hills and valleys on a map. These are your quilting lines.

Tip: Before you begin to quilt, cover your original photo with a plastic overlay. Use a whiteboard marker to draw the quilting lines you are planning. Draw lines about ⅛" apart, while you trace the bone structure of the face in the photo. Hang the photo with the overlay and take a picture of the drawn lines to verify they are correct. You can erase any of these lines with a tissue or a piece of batting. Now you can refer to this "road map" for your portrait while you are quilting it. You can also use a chalk pencil or sharpened blackboard chalk to draw temporary lines right on your quilt top.

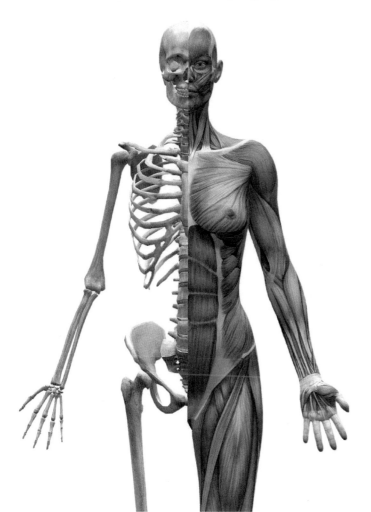

Here is "Danielle - Golden Tones," quilted according to the mapped contour lines. Cindy used thread that blended rather than contrasted with the fabrics.

"Danielle - Golden Tones," Cindy

In "La Campesina," notice the directionality of the stitching follows the contours of the face.

"La Campesina," Phyllis

"Peeper," Phyllis

Phyllis's quilt of "Peeper," with its close-ups, demonstrates how we quilt a young person.

This is a detail around the eyes of "Peeper." Notice the directionality of the stitching.

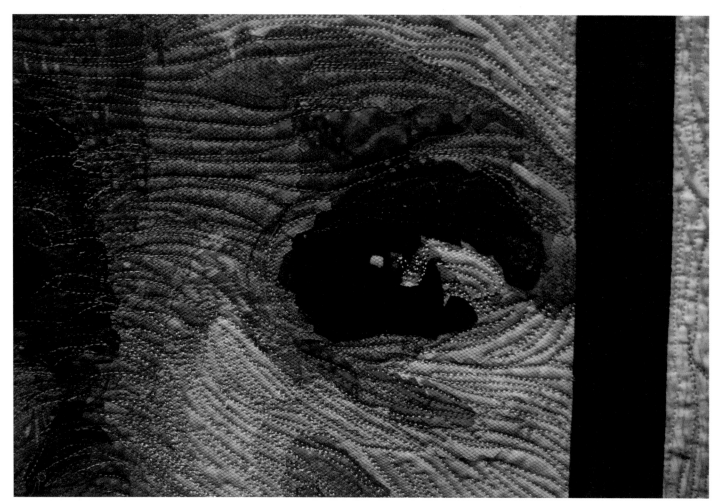

"Roger Chaffee, OBM," Phyllis

Well-chosen thread colors that match the values and colors of the layers enable the quilting lines to really blend in, as in "Roger Chaffee, OBM."

Quilting the Features

Skin

Skin acts like loose clothing. If the subject has loose skin, substantial fat deposits, or abnormal tension of the underlying soft tissue, then the quilting lines follow the furrows, contouring over the hills and valleys just like a draped cloth.

Lips

Lights and shadows on a face cause the area of the lips to be less defined so they almost disappear. Sometimes the sides of the lower lips recede into a single line or disappear altogether into the skin at the edges.

Here is a close-up of "Quilted Lips" based on a photo of Adina's lips. The values are correct, so it doesn't matter that they are purple. The quilting could have been done laterally, but since we wanted to emphasize their fullness, Cindy followed the muscles of the lips and quilted them with parallel, curved, vertical lines, using pinkish-tinted thread.

The thread choice is also based on value. By adding a touch of thread color in areas where the lips fade away, you can feel a hint of the shape. The skin surrounding the lips has been quilted laterally according to the shape of the face. This makes the lips stand out, because lateral stitching is perpendicular to the quilting direction of the lips.

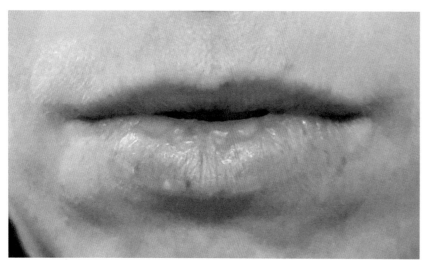

Note: In small art pieces it is more challenging to quilt mouths. One stitch can make a mouth look different. When it's a small piece, quilt the lines laterally across the lips.

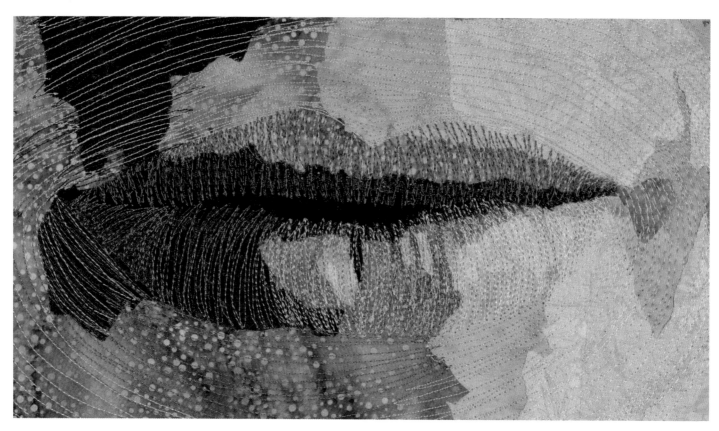

"Quilted Lips," Cindy

Making lips that are solid and symmetrical all around looks very "pasted-on" and unrealistic, like a comic book style. This is shown in the "Pasted-on Look" example.

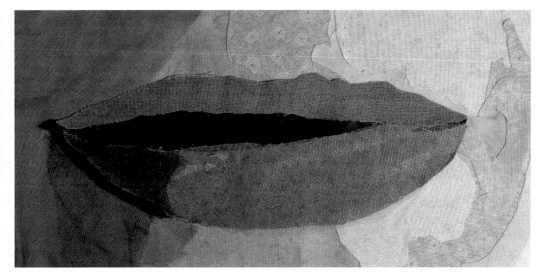

"Pasted-on Look," Cindy

Teeth

You can show a smile with teeth, so long as the teeth are cut out and quilted correctly. That makes all the difference. Teeth should not be contour quilted. Please, please do not outline them in dark thread, like a "piano mouth."

Quilt the lines between the teeth with thread that is the same color as the teeth. Typically, the color can vary from white, where the light hits the front of the mouth, to a darker color, often blue or purple, as the teeth recede into the back of the mouth on both sides.

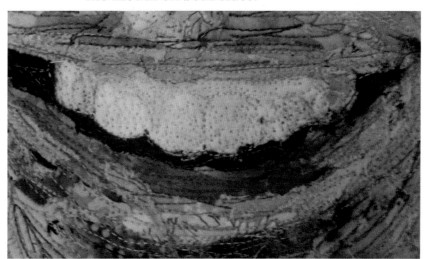

Baby teeth may be more widely separated. Even so, do not make the spaces between the teeth more than a few shades darker. Use a matching color to stitch around the teeth.

If your subject has severely discolored teeth, you may want to camouflage that a little bit by unifying the front teeth color and making the teeth a little lighter in value globally. Darken the teeth as they rotate to the side and back of the mouth.

The quilted teeth examples by Phyllis show what we have described here.

Notice how the teeth are quilted in the two versions of "Hula Kane." Since the teeth were very small in these tiny quilts, his very white teeth were cut out in one mass. Quilting consisted of using matching white thread to outline and define each tooth.

Detail of "Hula Kane," Phyllis

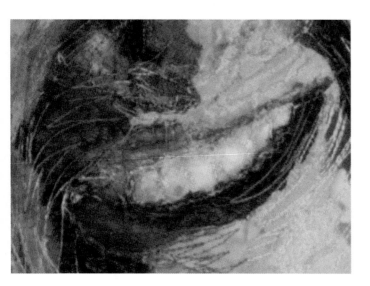

Detail of "Hula Kane 2," Phyllis

Eyes

When the eyes in your piece are small, just quilt along the contours of the curved lids. It's too difficult to accentuate more details.

In "Quilted Eyes," Cindy quilted a pair of Yosef's eyes. Look at the quilting lines inside each eye, especially in the close-up.

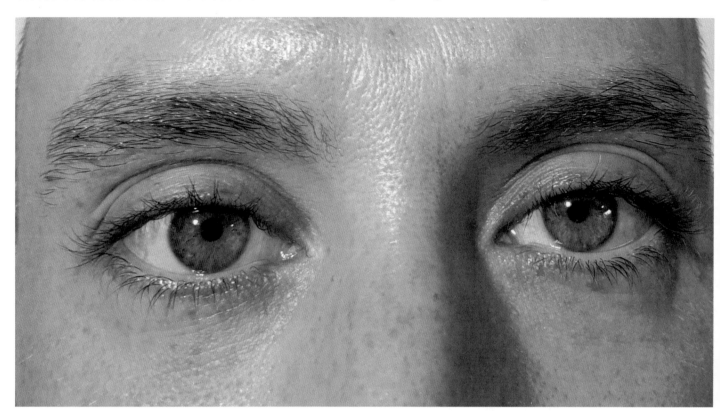

"Quilted Eyes," Cindy

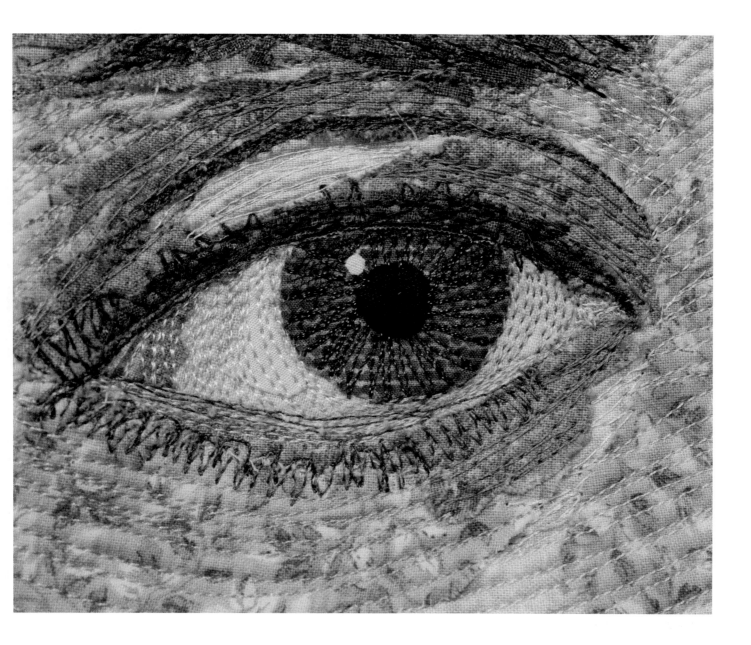

If the eyes are large, you can quilt a lot of detail. Refer to pp 15–17 in Chapter 2 to review the anatomy of an eye. The quilting lines should follow the round shape of the eyeball. Quilt the "whites" of the eye in elliptical lines on each side of the iris. These lines gradually get smaller as they approach the corners of the eye. Quilt the iris like a starburst from the pupil to the edge of the iris. Go all around the iris this way. Sew around the pupil with black thread.

Add a catchlight of white in the same location in both eyes (with white marker, paint, or thread),

where the light hits the eyes, so the eyes look alive. Shading and quilting in eyes creates volume. Without depth, eyes appear flat and look very cartoonish.

Quilt the inner lids and the outer lids with curved lines that follow the contour of the eye socket. These lateral lines are perpendicular to the whites of the eye. Finally, sew lashes and eyebrows according to your photo. Note the direction of the lashes and eyebrow hairs.

Quilts That Don't Follow Contour Lines

We've noticed that when traditional quilters create layered portraits with raw-edge applique, they question how to handle the unravelling raw edges. While quilting traditional projects, these quilters were taught to sew down all the edges of their applique patches. So they ask why they aren't doing the same in their art quilts.

Our answer is that when we create art, we have to think and create like an artist, not a seamstress. An artist would not expect to create a realistic effect if odd, non-anatomical lines were emphasized all over the portrait, just because the fabric pieces were cut that way. Nor would those lines help create the 3D features that realism demands. They create instead what we call the "Frankenstein effect" because of these scary, unwanted lines.

Tip: If you have stitched around the patches and are not happy with the result, you can improve the realistic effect by adding contour line quilting over the patches. The stitching around the patches may fade into the background. Next time remember the fusing and contour quilting are sufficient for holding down the patches.

In the following series, the same layered quilt that we saw posterized in Chapter 4 is quilted in four different ways. In our opinion, only the last result enhances the 3D effect we are promoting. You have artistic license to follow the other three results, but they would not be our choice.

The first one outlines the features, coloring book style. The result is a cartoon effect.

1. Outlined features

The second is quilted randomly with no regard to contours or shapes. It could be swirls, straight lines, meanders or feathers.

2. Random quilting

The third version shows stitching around the patches irrespective of the anatomy of the subjects.

3. Quilting around the patches

The fourth example, "Holding You," which is quilted using contour lines, is the method we feel best accentuates the realistic effect.

Having now explained our position, we do want to say, we aren't the "quilt police." We realize that there are many different opinions as to the best way to quilt faces. We applaud everyone's varying approaches. If your style is not realistic, you can free motion any contour pattern you want, such as meandering swirls and loops.

"Holding You," Dassi Shani Pintar

Quilted Layered Collages

These are the quilts that we described step by step in Chapter 6. The Layered Collage, "Jeanne," is quilted along contour lines.

Here again, on the **right** is the unquilted version.

Below is the quilted layered collage.

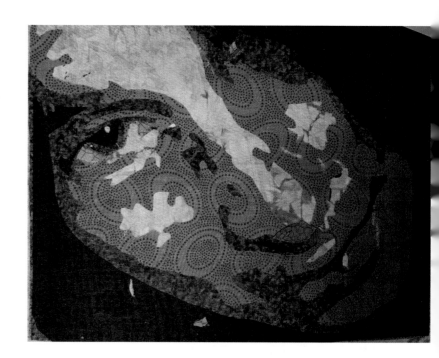

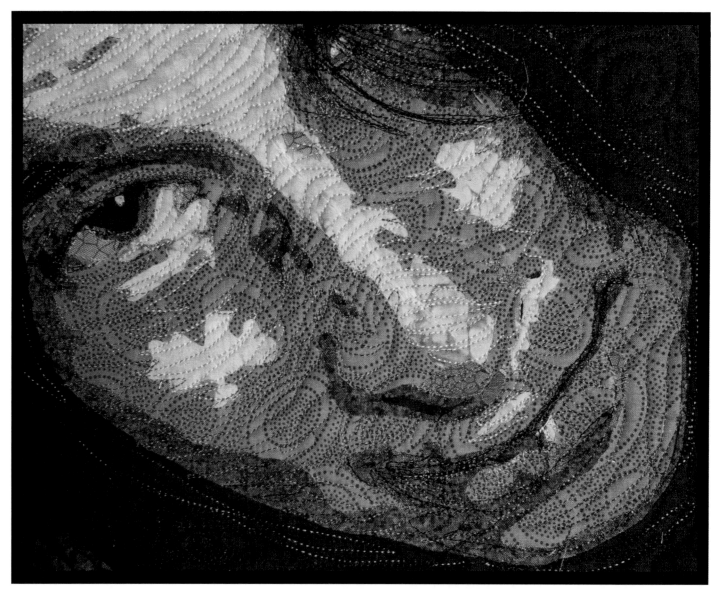

Quilted layered collage, "Jeanne," Phyllis

For "Scrappy Dan" (Scrappy Collage Technique) only, the rules are just a bit different. Because the busy-ness of all the scraps obscures some of the definition of the features, we recommend quilting exterior contour lines to outline the features in addition to quilting interior contour lines.

Quilt around the head, and along the edges of the features. You can use variegated thread to blend all the fabrics, and generally do contour quilting to accentuate the 3D effect. Because of all the busy printed fabrics the quilting will not show as much as in the layered technique.

If you are using a domestic machine, it's a good idea

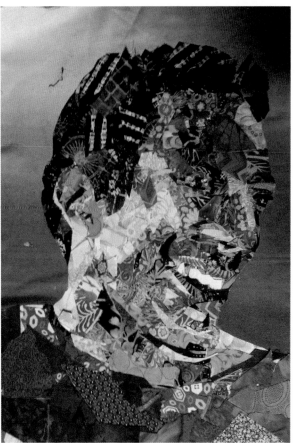

to quilt from the center, smoothing out the tulle as you widen your area so there are no folds. The tulle color will simply blend into the pattern and will not change the overall look.

The scrappy, unquilted version is **above**.

The scrappy, quilted version is on the **left**.

Quilted scrappy collage, "Scrappy Dan," Phyllis

8 Emphasis on Texture

An advantage of fabric over other art media is that fabric is textured. There is the implied texture in a printed, striped or plaid fabric, or even one printed to look like a textured weave. There are also the actual textures of fabrics at our disposal. Velvets with dense upright fibers that absorb light and produce a mysterious darkness can be used for an animal's furry coat. Sheer fabrics create an airy effect. Rayon (aka viscose) typically comes in vibrant, reflective colors and has a beautiful drape.

Integrating actual and implied textures in a scene enhances its realistic effect. By using a bumpy burlap for a sack, shimmery, shiny silk for curtains, rich velvet for a sofa, or pleating for drapes, a scene becomes more convincing. In addition, there are many special qualities to fabric like the tightness of the weave, which cause it to be opaque and stiff. Looser weaves result in a soft and flowing, more transparent cloth that immediately conjures up movement. These can be used to simulate water and reflected light.

Textile artists can add more depth and volume by using the variety of textured fabrics available. A stone wall with crevices or wrinkles on an older face can be achieved by mixing fibers and textures with different values in an organic way. Adding layers of dark tulle, which is semi-transparent, gives the impression of shadows without changing the color of the underlying fabric. We can add sparkle and shimmer with organza and Angelina® fibers, and bling like beads and sequins. Really, there is no end to the creativity.

When we use these fabrics to make portraits, we have an opportunity to elevate the character of our quilted work to a more "mixed-media, fine art" approach.

Several of our colleagues specialize in one form or another of textured work, so we are including them in our book.

We use cheesecloth for lots of effects, but Mary Pal takes it to a whole new level. She is well known for her exquisite fabric portraits, made entirely of cheesecloth, achieving values by varying the density of the cheesecloth. Mary worked from a photograph, taken by Csaba Zoller for her art, "Trusting." She remembers how she looked at it and wondered how she could use white cheesecloth to differentiate the overlapping elements: scarf, hair, skin. It required some careful sculpting. The results are amazing.

This is the portrait, "Trusting."

"Trusting," Mary Pal
Photo Credit: Ray Pilon
Reference Photo: Csaba Zoller

By just using layers of white cheesecloth, Mary approximates the features and impact of black & white photography, along with the textured effect of fabric. It is truly a unique style.

Notice the detail around the eyes in Mary Pal's close-up of the "Lighthouse Keeper." Again, all the detail was achieved solely with layers of cheesecloth.

Detail of "Lighthouse Keeper," Mary Pal
Photo Credit: Ray Pilon
Reference Photo: Alan Kingsbury

Phyllis was fortunate enough to take a class with Mary and created a quilt featuring Itzhak Perlman using the cheesecloth technique.

"Virtuoso," Phyllis

Hiyam Salman uses burlap and other unconventional materials to create a uniquely styled portrait of her husband.

"My Husband," Hiyam Salman

This beautiful image by Geneviève Attinger is created with layered values for realism and then thread painted to create an extremely smooth surface, enabling our attention to be directed to the woman's mysterious expression and the starkly contrasting texture of the twine.

"La Discrète," Geneviève Attinger

77

Hala Al-Osailan has created a woven tapestry. Notice the woven strands that are so expertly combined to form the features of this woman's face.

"Tapestry," Hala Al-Osailan

"Phoenician Beauty," Mary Wood Tabar

Virtual texture can be accomplished in many ways. Here, Shoshi Rimer's homage to the mosaic style simulates ceramic tiles.

The texture in this piece by Mary Wood Tabar is created by the fanciful quilting and the stripes. The eye and lips, which are not quilted, look alive due to the catchlights. Notice that the stripes and swirly quilting do not detract from the believability of the face because of the beautiful iris and pupil. The artist has definitely put her own artistic spin on this face.

"Mona Lisa of the Galilee," Shoshi Rimer

This felted portrait by Valerie Dunne creates a soft, tactile surface that is consistent with the softness of her daughter's face.

It is created with wool roving rather than fabric. The wool can be wet felted and/or needle felted, and fine detail can be obtained. In essence, it's a painting with bits of dyed wool rather than dabs of paint. The felting process adheres the wool to the base, and quilting is not needed for structure, but could be added for additional texture.

Stile Malena has used tiny snippets of fabric covered with netting to create this textured portrait.

The fabric is slashed into confetti-like pieces that are separated by color and then dropped into place. Divisions between the colors are blurred by blending the snippets. The netting or tulle keeps the bits of fabric in place, and quilting can be done directly over the tulle to add even more texture. The effect is very soft and blended, like an oil painting.

"Portrait of Amy," Valerie Dunne

"Beatrice Portinari," Stile Malena (Laura Franci)

Bella Kaplan's minimalist rendition whispers a suggestion of a woman's face. We, the viewers, fill in the blanks.

"A Tribute to John," Meena Schaldenbrand

"Manya Shochat," Bella Kaplan

Jack Edson's monumentally sized face is composed of actual, traditional, pieced quilt blocks, which are arranged according to value to create a portrait.

Meena Schaldenbrand's pixelated construction technique creates a somewhat abstract but still recognizable rendering of her subject. The effect is slightly blurred, as though the person is there, but maybe not fully in attendance. Quilting lines would detract from the emphasis on the pixels.

"Charles E. Burchfield," Jack Edson

Sandra Bruce didn't know Justice Ginsburg personally, but she, like many of us, wanted to celebrate one of the greatest women of our time. She obtained permission and created, in her own style, a lovely tribute piece to Ruth Bader Ginsburg, z"l.

The smooth texture is created by piecing squares of appropriate value in a manner reminiscent of large pixels. This technique is called Matrix Quilting.

"The Notorious RBG," Sandra Bruce
Original reference photo by AP with permission

Possibly the ultimate in contour quilting is present in the work of several artists who create layered or collage applique images and then quilt such closely spaced lines that we call it thread painting, or thread sketching. Marilyn Wall's piece of her granddaughter is an example of fine thread painting.

"Hannah," Marilyn H. Wall

Speaking of creating a mood and expressing a spirit, let's move on.

9 Heart and Soul

The sky might have been dreary and overcast, but this little one felt that a day at the beach was heavenly.

And now we get to the heart of the "why." It is generally agreed that the purpose of art is to communicate our feelings about our subject. Thus far in this book we have delved into the "nuts and bolts" of creating a portrait. It is our conviction that a thorough understanding of anatomy and a mastery of the tools of creating an illusion are essential to producing art. We must master the tools that enable us to communicate the core, emotional fundamentals of our vision.

A portrait becomes a work of art when the artist has conveyed his or her understanding of the subject to the viewer, and the viewer is able to derive the essence and the position of the subject in the universe. There is an active engagement between the artist and the viewer to tell a story.

The story unfolds in many ways. We learn about the background and setting from the accompanying "props," the lighting, which conveys the time of day and the season, and the physical location and general context.

Likewise, the colors and textures of the face and hair suggest the subject's gender, ethnicity, age, attention to hygiene, and state of health. The subject's clothing may tell us something about the person's profession, hobbies, and passions.

The story is especially portrayed by the expressions on the subject's face, by the laugh lines, the skin furrows, the body language, the tilt of the head, the angle of the jaw, the tightness of the mouth, the position of the hands, and a thousand other little things. But it is also conveyed by our choices of values, colors, textures, composition, etc.

In this portrait of a musician friend, in addition to his obvious concentration on the guitar, Phyllis added the right props to elicit the viewer's reaction that this piece gets in our town. "Yes, that is definitely Timm!"

"Java Jive," Phyllis

of the person. Heck, we can just print someone else's photo on fabric and stitch a few lines around the features, and get the resulting work accepted into art quilt exhibits. (It's been done!)

But is it art? Does it convey **our** message? Does it come from **our** soul?

No.

That's right.

No.

We can modify or outright use someone else's painting or drawing as a basis for our work and still believe we are creating our own great art. We should not delude ourselves. **That is not our art.**

A police sketch artist need not convey emotion, just an exact rendition of features. But if we do the same, we will be lacking

It is true that a portrait quilt can be created by choosing an existing photo, posterizing it, and perhaps choosing to use the colors generated by the computer program. We can even use a photo (copyright free) from sources and collaborate with the original photographer, who did the work of positioning, lighting, draping and eliciting the desired expression from the subject.

We may or may not select and edit the features of that photo, and we may create a very credible, though obviously thoroughly derivative likeness

something. Not the "what" but the "why"—the soul and meaning of our subject. We will not allow the subject to express his or her message. We will silence his/her voice.... And our own!

Creating a portrait is more than snapping a picture. It requires artistic skill to position, elicit an expression, adjust the lighting, etc. to share our understanding of our subject—his or her personality, mood and thoughts. We share this with viewers who can then react to our feelings about our subject.

This quilt is a portrait of Dr. Quentin Young, Phyllis's mentor and medical director at Cook County Hospital, where Phyllis was an intern. Dr. Young fought tirelessly for the rights of all to have health care. He marched with Martin Luther King Jr. (and was his physician), and he lent medical presence and support at virtually every march, rally, protest, and activity for civil rights and human rights. He inspired many of us to serve the needy from ghettos at home to third world countries.

"Nobody Out," Phyllis

Sometimes our work depicts individuals who are no longer with us, or whom we cannot photograph ourselves, but wish to honor or memorialize. Maybe we just draw our own interpretations, as Phyllis did in this piece for a Studio Art Quilt Associates (SAQA) show called "Text Messages." Phyllis's vision of Moses' face seemed appropriate to her. In addition, she notes the messages on his tablets, unlike those on an iPad, were truly written in stone.

"Early Tablets," Phyllis

If we want to use photos of a known figure as our inspiration, we have to start with photos or paintings or drawings or descriptions created by others and then collaborate with those artists. In this case it is even more crucial that we go beyond merely downloading a photo and reproducing it. We must research our subject, see what that person said and what others said about him/her, assess our own reactions and feelings about that individual, and then depict the essence of that person with our chosen values, colors and textures. It is our reactions and choices in this regard that enable us to project our own emotions into our art.

This quilt is part of a series honoring Apollo astronauts. Rather than a bland depiction of a man in front of a spaceship, Phyllis looked more deeply into his story. Dr Edgar Mitchell, who had earned a PhD in astrophysics and was a NASA Apollo astronaut, returned from space claiming that "aliens prevented World War III." He was quite adamant about that and created the Noetic society. He travelled the country to explain his views.

Phyllis therefore felt that she had to depict his portrait complete with his guardian aliens! The portrait Phyllis used as her inspiration for the astronaut's face was taken from the NASA website, which expressly allowed use of their publicity photos for any purpose. Be sure you have permission to use a picture you find on the Internet!

"Dr. Mitchell and Friends," Phyllis

When someone looks at our portrait and admires how correctly we depicted the hair patterns and eye shapes and length of the nose, etc. and notices that it looks "just like him," we are of course pleased, but as artists we should not be satisfied. What we want to hear is, "Yes, that's Uncle Ed! You've captured his curmudgeonly exterior, and that twinkle in his eye gives him away!" They aren't sure how you did it. Perhaps it was by using warm colors and lighting. Maybe it was the shiny thread in the eye. But, you did it. You were able to create that emotional response. It's what the viewer feels or senses, not what the critic analyzes, that tells us we have communicated what we wanted to say.

This work of Cindy's is called "Blooming." This self-portrait was photographed right before the birth of her first child. You can glean the carefree spirit and pure happiness in this scene.

"Blooming," Cindy

In this piece, a grandmother is lighting candles for the Sabbath. Hanging on the wall in the background is a charcoal portrait by her granddaughter. In the scene, the woman's late husband and the puppets are indeed "watching over" her. Memorializing the story of this photo was very important to the family. When the family was presented with the quilt, they were moved to tears. They said Cindy's quilt captured the essence of the subjects and particularly "'nailed' the glow of Dad's face!" The special setting, the covered face, and the wall art all tell a story that is especially meaningful to the recipients of this piece.

"Sabbath," Cindy

Original charcoal portrait, "My Special Grandpa" by Tali Perlman Ohana
Reference Photo: Alissa Perlman

Here are two portraits of everyday life by Cindy.

This market scene with its colors, smells, sounds, and flavor is typical of the Jerusalem Market. This unique place engages our senses and our palettes.

Below, Cindy's family photo shows only the family's legs and feet. It immediately evokes an image of warmth, togetherness, home and hearth. In other words, sometimes less is more. You don't always have to tell the whole story. The viewer can work out the details.

"Colors of the Jerusalem Market," Cindy

"Put Up Your Feet and Take It Easy," Cindy

87

The choice of values conveys the mood. A close (low or even dark contrast) set of values evokes a somber mood. A full range of high contrast values elicits dynamic excitement. A high-key, or generally light-valued portrait conveys

"Budding Sensibilities," Cindy

delicacy, innocence, enjoyment of a bright spring day.

Cindy's portrait of her grandson smelling a flower uses high-key values to emphasize the innocence of a child.

To the right is a quilt featuring the joy of this mother and daughter pair. Because the girl loves spinning objects, spirals and circles were incorporated into the quilting.

"Encircled with Love,"
Madhu Mathur
Quilted by Helen Godden

88

A low-key or dark-valued portrait can indicate a thoughtful man of substance, who is carrying the weight of great decisions on his shoulders, or is perhaps burdened with a sense of melancholy or dark thoughts.

Color choices can indicate ambient conditions, but can also go beyond that and convey the warmth or coolness of the subject's emotional state and personality. Using reds for warmth and blues for coolness are universally understood.

The dark values and somber colors in Phyllis's "Night Terror" enhances the feeling that the subject is very afraid and in great danger.

Sometimes a portrait doesn't have to show the face at all. Sometimes the body language tells the story, as we can see by the young man in the lower corner of the piece, "Death of Science."

However, Phyllis admits the story is pretty straightforward when one of the subjects has a knife in his back!

"Death of Science," Phyllis

"Night Terror," Phyllis

Texture and pattern choices can suggest more aspects of the subject's personality. Heavy fabric may suggest ruggedness, while lively patterns and colors may convey a warm and engaging personality. Shiny, neutral fabric suggests a cool and sophisticated persona. Dark fabric that absorbs light may suggest depression. The list of possible choices goes on and on. Each color, value, and texture should be chosen thoughtfully to indicate our emotional response to the person in the portrait.

Fabric artistry affords us advantages over painters. We can use texture, pattern, design, thread types and colors, and the style of quilting, whether lightheartedly swirly or realistically contoured, to help us communicate.

There's a whole world of different artistic styles and genres to express emotional content, from abstract to impressionistic, from cartoon to cubist. But as we said, the rules don't matter if you like the effect you've created. There are many portraits that succeed as art in spite of the fanciful quilting lines. Follow your heart on this! Once you know the rules, you can follow them, or break them. We grant you an Artistic License, duly and officially awarded.

Phyllis created a series of cubist portraits. This one, called "Pursuit of La Paloma," strives to recreate the emotion of the spurned lover, despite its distinctly non-realist style.

The colors used to create the unfortunate suitor express his rage and frustration. When we create fabric portraits in styles other than realistic, often we don't care about creating a likeness (though it can still be done, of course, with rather wild prints, and quilted realistically). In that case, the quilting style can be any pattern of the artist's choosing and should enhance the style or genre.

"Pursuit of La Paloma,"
Phyllis

90

Birgit Ruotsala created an evocative mood with her pen and ink, minimalist drawing, filled in with tight thread painting, so as not to detract from the spareness of the almost monotone image. The unusual pose draws full attention to the legs of the ballerina.

This thread sketch by Kathy Mullaney demonstrates that a simple drawing without shading can evoke a warm response when the subject is the love between a person and pet.

"Puppy Love," Kathy Mullaney

"Grace on Point," Birgit Ruotsala

This subject focused on his phone rather than noticing his surroundings while walking the streets of a frenetic NYC.

"Connected," Suzanne Munroe

Everyday life has a distinctive flavor in each place.

Here a generous flower vendor shares with a child.

"Anjalè," Chitra Mandanna

The joy is apparent in this thread painted face by Joan Davis.

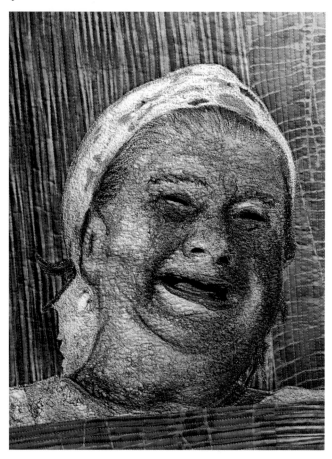

"Busha," Joan Davis

This woman from the central part of Nepal is old, but she may be younger than she looks.

"The Nepalese Woman," Dorte Jensen

This quilt tells a story about a girl on an Indian reservation.

"If Birds Fly Over the Rainbow,
Why Oh Why Can't I," Becky Erdman
Inspired by a painting by Karen Noles

The title of this quilt and the subject's blank look describes the story: "If I Could Wish One Thing, I'd Hear You Call My Name."

This quilt is a thread painting of a nun covering her face with her hands.

"Nun," Milla Malchow

*"If I Could Wish One Thing,
I'd Hear You Call My Name,"
Suzanne Quinones*

This older couple is in a comforting embrace. Perhaps they are dancing.

The subject, who has an engaging, piercing look, seems to be smiling back at us.

"Iris & Schep Portrait," Roxane Lessa

*"Untitled," Lynn Czaban
Reference Photo: Library of Congress,
Prints & Photographs Division FSA/OWI
Collection, (LC-USF33-T01-002325-M3)*

93

This piece by Phyllis expresses glee mixed with slight hesitancy at the "Petting Zoo."

"Petting Zoo,"
Phyllis

And who has not experienced an exhausted child misbehaving at the supermarket, as captured by Kathleen Kastles?

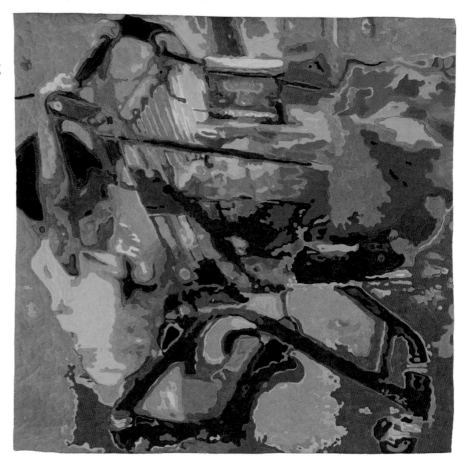

"Exhaustion," Kathleen Kastles
Photo Credit: José Morales, Xinia
Productions, Maui, HI

Tamar Drucker created this quilt to memorialize letters her grandfather used to send her family from overseas when she was growing up. The quilt incorporates the text of his last remaining letter together with fabrics that looked like postcards. In the foreground her grandfather is blowing a shofar (ram's horn) for the Jewish high holidays.

"Letters from My Grandfather,"
Tamar Drucker

Tina Sommer Paaske charmed us with a quilt of her grandson, who proudly flaunted a black eye and a missing tooth after attending football camp.

Storytelling creates the bond between the artist and the viewer. There is nothing more personal than a portrait. Make it so!

We can't end this chapter without recommending three collections curated by Susanne Miller Jones that include scores of portrait stories. These books are: "Fly Me to the Moon," "HERstory," and "OURstory."

"Mathias," Tina Sommer Paaske

10 Care for Your Hands

(Now speaking as Phyllis Cullen, MD)

Before we add the final details, we wanted to address an issue that seems to affect many of us, especially as we age. Since it may be a limiting factor and may prevent us from even being creative, we need to talk about our hands.

Book Two will discuss in great detail the hazards, pitfalls, and ergonomics of quilting. However, as a physician specializing in chronic pain management, as well as someone with arthritis of the hands, Phyllis felt we needed to include some advice on dealing with a few of the most common hand ailments: basal joint arthritis (causing thumb pain and stiffness) and carpal tunnel syndrome (causing pain, weakness and numbness).

Thumb Arthritis

This includes osteoarthritis, rheumatoid arthritis, post-traumatic injuries, sprains, dislocations, and repetitive strain. The first place many of us notice joint pain is on the side of the hand, halfway between the wrist and where the thumb exits from the palm.

Splints: Use of a splint may provide support and improve hand function. There are several different types with varying degrees of stiffness. Some splints allow you to work while supporting the joints; others are quite rigid and force you to rest your hands. There are soft splints and compression-elastic Ace™ wrap-type gloves, which may or may not have a bendable metal support along the thumb, that can be used while you are working. At night or when not crafting, wearing a rigid or custom-made splint that holds the thumb away from the palm may help rest the joint at the base of the thumb and reduce inflammation.

Exercises: Avoid exercises that involve pinching, gripping or squeezing, because these actions can aggravate inflammation, tendonitis, and arthritis. However, maintaining flexibility by touching your thumb to the base of the pinky, opening and closing the fingers, gently stretching fingers, and/or grasping and squeezing the base of the thumb may be helpful.

Hot and cold treatments are a mainstay. Start with ice for acute sprains and overuse (unless you have Raynaud's).
If the hand is swollen, try cold. Otherwise various forms of heat often relieve stiffness and pain. Warm water, heating pads, and especially paraffin baths may be very helpful, though the relief will be temporary.

Topical treatments are available. Lidocaine patches can be used to numb painful areas. Use only those specially formulated to penetrate intact skin, not gels or liquids. Capsaicin can block pain signals. Salicylates are mildly anti-inflammatory. Cannabidiol (CBD) may interrupt pain signals. Anti-inflammatory gels, like Voltaren®, often help reduce inflammation. You can consult with your doctor about these choices.

Other therapies: TENS Units (Transcutaneous Electrical Nerve Stimulation), light treatments, occupational therapy, refraining from lifting heavy pots and pans, as well as not using buttons and zippers all may help.

Rest your hands when they start to hurt. Take a break during repetitive tasks.

Oral anti-inflammatories can be helpful but come with some risks.

Anti-inflammatory foods and supplements, however, seem pretty safe. Eat fresh fruits/vegetables and whole grains. Avoid sugar and processed foods. For some people avoiding gluten seems to help. You may want to try supplementing with glucosamine, chondroitin, cinnamon, turmeric, and ginger. Many people find them helpful.

Use the right tools. One important thing we can do is choose the right tools or modify the ones we have. The object is to avoid pinching, twisting, and gripping as much as possible. So try using: non-slip rulers, padded rotary-cutter handles, sharp rotary-cutter blades, finger pads to grip hand needles, tool handles wrapped with batting, raised tables for cutting and coloring, electric scissors, cutting machines, spring-loaded scissors that pop open after cutting, and quilting gloves for better traction.

If all these suggestions don't alleviate your pain, visit a pain doctor. Doctors can inject steroids, or non-steroidal anti-inflammatories, opioids, hyaluronic acid, platelet-rich plasma, or various other substances to heal the joint. Surgery specifically for arthritis in the hands is a last resort.

Carpal (and Cubital) Tunnel Syndrome

This includes other nerve and tendon entrapments.

For carpal tunnel syndrome, besides the ideas offered for arthritis, night splints seem to offer the greatest relief. Stretching, steroid injections, braces, etc. may also offer relief for a while. However, in Dr. Phyllis's opinion, carpal tunnel should be treated by a simple surgery before the compressed nerve dies. Tight scar-like tissue bands as in Dupuytrens and trigger-fingers can be surgically released.

Let's be kind to our hands. We need them to last!

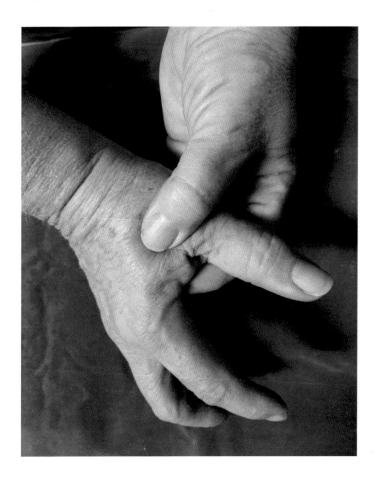

Getting Back to the Portrait: Final Details

Details are the flare that turn a great work into a masterpiece. Once you add a dab here or a highlight there, the difference is suddenly night and day. We have compiled some suggestions that can elevate your work to amazing.

Darkening and Shading

Remember lips fit over teeth. Because lips form a convex shape, there is always a dark line between them, which may be rendered as a broken, irregular, thick or thin line, but not as a straight even line.

We can shade areas that require a darker value with ink, paint, marker, colored pencil, tulle, organza or anything else that gets the job done. There are no rules saying these light and dark details have to be created with fabric pieces. If a dark line is needed or you missed some eyelashes, draw them with a marker, preferably one that won't bleed. Try Uni-Posca Paint Marker Pens™, which are acrylic, or Pentel EnerGel® ink fabric markers, or Sakura® Pigma Micron pens for fabric. Tsukineko® Fabrico® Markers are also good alternatives for shading and making fine lines. Our experience is that Sharpie® markers can smear and fade.

We have tried lots of products. We use markers, gelly pens, glitter, beads, Derwent® Inktense pencils and blocks, watercolors, thickened dyes, acrylics, pastels, oil paint sticks, colored pencils, etc. Try your hand at different solutions to add your own touch to your work.

Each product has setting instructions, which should be followed carefully. Heat setting with a hot iron is common for many pencils and dyes. Some dyes mix with water to achieve richer colors. Some can be fugitive, fade, wash away, etc., if not fixed to fabric with some sort of textile medium. Some fabric paints or markers are already treated with textile medium and need no further attention once applied to fabric.

Prismacolor Premier® pencils are soft pencils that work well on fabric. Caran d'Ache® pencils are a little harder but also work well on fabric. If you combine Caran d'Ache® Neocolor® II crayons with water, the color will deepen and smooth out. Without adding a textile medium or aloe to Neocolor II crayons, the color will bleed.

Synthetic fabrics like tulle and organza will melt with a hot iron. They can be fused with a cooler iron, but cover them with a parchment sheet or a silicon sheet to protect them while pressing. You can also sew them in place.

Lights and Highlights

We use a white-out pen or a drop of white acrylic paint to add the catchlight to the iris of both eyes. Amazingly, this spot of white transforms eyes so they look alive.

To brighten an area, we can use light colored overlays, white ink, or white paints.

White lines can be added with a Uni-ball® Signo gel pen. You may have to go over it several times, as it seems to fade into the fabric. For really white lines, use a Uni-Posca marker pen or a Marabu Graphix® Sketch Marker.

You can use a glitter gel pen to add a colored reflection or sparkle to an eye. Try a color like aqua, turquoise or blue. And if there are clothes or jewelry included in your portrait, the sky's the limit for what you can add.

Surface Design and Embellishment

Embroidery thread is another great way to embellish. Learning embroidery stitching is a whole other world to explore. Add beads, crystals, sequins, and buttons to the mix to liven up a surface. Remember though, that hard objects are difficult to quilt around, so add them after quilting.

Trimming Your Quilt

After cleaning up the threads on the front and the back, trim the quilt. There are a number of modern tools that help with this process, especially on large quilts. Beba's L-shaped rotary rulers can help you square the corners. Beba's also makes extra-long rotary rulers, so you don't have to move the ruler while trimming a long side.

Double laser lights with beams that form an L are also very helpful. By lining up the quilt with the beams, your cuts will be straight and accurate.

Binding

We will preface this by saying quilts don't have to be rectangular. They can be unusual shapes. But if a quilt is more conventional, facing or binding are the typical choices. One can also zigzag the edges. Let your quilt dictate how you finish. Traditional judges will prefer that you machine-sew the binding on the front and hand-sew the back, so the stitches don't show on the front. Neatness counts.

Photographing Your Finished Quilt

So, we have taken you to the end of the story for now. You've finished your quilt. Now you need to take a really high-quality photo of the entire quilt and a close-up. That is, if you want to show off your quilt.

Here are some tips about taking photos of your finished quilts.
- Make sure the lighting is daylight quality, which is the 6000K range.
- Pin the quilt on a design wall and use a tripod to take the photos.
- Ideally, a good camera with a macro lens will produce the best result.
- Image resolution should be 300 ppi for

print, which means there are 300 pixels in every square inch of your image. You can check resolution if you right click on an image and select **Properties** > **Details**. The higher the resolution, the better the photo.

Take a few full shots and then check the quality on your computer. Zoom in to 100% and make sure the photo is clear and that you can see the stitching.

To take a few close-up shots, go back to the camera and move the tripod closer to the quilt. Don't crop the close-up from the full shot. Check the close-ups for clarity. You should be able to see stitches very well.

If you send these photos to be judged, the judges will do this process as well. They are looking to see your work at 100%.

Always email your files as attachments. Do not embed them in your email. Other methods of sending images may compress the files.

Gifting

We like approval and seeing our work shown and appreciated. One of the nicest gestures and the best feeling we will ever experience is to gift a quilt to someone. People love portraits of their family or themselves, as you can see in "Dale's Gift."

"Dale's Gift," Phyllis

Judging

We quilt because we love the medium. We love working with fabrics, and as funny as it sounds, some of us love cutting up fabric so we can put it back together in a totally different arrangement. Sometimes, we also quilt for the sake of showing our work to a larger audience in prestigious shows, because we enjoy the affirmation from judges and viewers of our successful portrayals. Maybe winning 1st place prizes is an ego boosting goal. To that end, we are including a brief discussion about what judges look for. And perhaps we will all produce higher quality work.

Here are some judging criteria we heard at one quilt show:

- Contemporary quilting should be based on, but not limited to, the skills associated with traditional quilting.
- Any fabric, notion, form of construction or embellishment used in non-traditional quilting should be appropriate for its genre.
- Creative design and effective use of color are of the highest order of importance.

Judges want to see that WOW factor. Does that quilt "knock their socks off"? Originality counts here. The idea for the quilt should be yours.

They look at the composition and fabric choices. How exciting is the design? Is there movement and harmony? Do the fabric colors blend well together? Do the thread choices work well with the composition? Does the thread blend with the back of the quilt? How well is the work made? Is it finished off neatly? Does the binding enhance the quilt? Is it straight and evenly quilted throughout? Is the stitch tension uniform throughout?

In other words, the judges look at workmanship. They look at the backs of the quilts and do want to see the stitching and buried knots. That might be too much for some of us, but if you really want a ribbon in a quilt show, as opposed to an art contest, you'll need to consider their requirements.

Coming Soon! Book Two

If you're still with us, we know you're off to a great start. But the fact is, the journey has just begun.

We have some new great material to share. In Book Two we'll explore more fun ways to make faces, besides digging deeper into drawing, studying full figures, backgrounds and compositions, more about photography, ergonomics, and much more.

By looking at portraits done in many different styles, genres, and techniques throughout history, we'll show how portraiture evolved and what's happening today. We'll see very different types of portraits, like Phyllis's surreal creation and a lot of guest artists working in many, many different styles.

"Just Surreal," Phyllis

Then we will explore animals, because we know how we all love portraying the furry members of our families. We'll learn the ins and outs of animal anatomy: hair, fur, and expressions.

Here are a few photos to give you an idea of what's to come.

How about these cat eyes by Phyllis?

Detail of "Buddy," Phyllis

Or this thread painted furry friend by Cindy?

Detail of "Couch of Cats," Cindy

And "Shorty" done as a scrappy collage by Phyllis?

"Shorty," Phyllis

There'll be loads of animals in other styles, done by other great artists as well, and some more great stories.

Watch out for Book Two in early 2021. Also, join our Facebook group: It's All About the Face (https://www.facebook.com/groups/itsallabouttheface) to share what you've created and for more inspiration.

We never run out of ideas when we bring people and animals to life in our quilts!

List of Works

Made in the USA
Las Vegas, NV
18 February 2021